SIMPLE GUIDE TO

SIKHISM

Sewa Singh Kalsi

D1146501

GLOBAL BOOKS LTD

ABOUT THE AUTHOR

SEWA SINGH KALSI is a lecturer in Sikh Studies in the Department of Theology and Religious Studies at the University of Leeds. He has published widely on the development of the Sikh tradition in Britain, and is author of *The Evolution of a Sikh Community in Britain* (University of Leeds, 1992). He is a member of the British Association for the Study of Religions, and the Punjab Research Group, UK.

Khanda   Ek-Onkar

Khanda: Literally a double-edged sword, it denotes the Sikh emblem which has a *Khanda* in the centre surrounded by a circle called *Chokkar* and two swords. This symbol of Sikhism may be seen on the *Nishan Sahib* (Sikh flag)

Ek-Onkar: One of the popular symbols in Sikhism; it is composed of two words – **Ek** (one) and **Onkar** (God). It is found at the beginning of the Mulmantra in the Adi Granth

DRAWINGS BY
IRENE SANDERSON

SIMPLE GUIDE TO

SIKHISM

Simple Guides ● Series 3
WORLD RELIGIONS

The Simple Guide to
SIKHISM
By Sewa Singh Kalsi

First published 1999 by
GLOBAL BOOKS LTD
PO Box 219, Folkestone, Kent CT20 3LZ

© 1999 Global Books Ltd

ISBN 1-86034-063-6

British Library Cataloguing in Publication Data
A CIP catalogue entry for this book
is available from the British Library

Set in Futura 10½ on 11½ point by Bookman, Hayes, Middlesex
Printed and bound in Malta by Interprint Ltd.

Contents

MAP OF INDIA

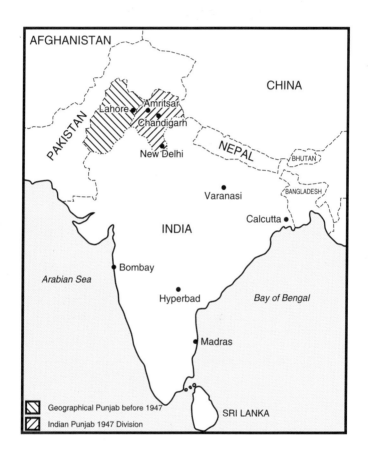

Foreword

The existence of Sikh communities throughout the world presents a fascinating story of an immigrant community which originated in the Punjab, India, more than five hundred years ago. As everyone knows, male Sikhs are easily recognized by their turbans and beards. (But, remember, not all men wearing turbans are Sikhs!) Over the centuries, they have acquired a reputation for being sturdy, hard-working and adventurous; they are a people who have earned the reputation for being extremely brave and loyal soldiers. They have also become known for being a militant people.

Although the Sikh tradition evolved in the Punjab region, a significant migration of Sikhs to overseas countries took place during the period of British rule (1757-1947), but particularly after the Second World War. It is also worth noting that the Sikhs' impact on the religious, social, economic and political map of modern India is far more significant than their numerical strength would suggest, bearing in mind that Sikhs make up only two per cent of the population of India today. The overwhelming proportion of Sikhs, of course, live in the Punjab and belong to Punjabi families.

This *Simple Guide to Sikhism* can at best be only an introduction to the subject; nevertheless, it attempts to address a wide variety of basic questions such as 'Who are the Sikhs? Where have they come from? And what are their religious beliefs and practices?' As for the Sikh diaspora, it surely underlines the capacity of Sikh migrants to restructure their traditional cultural institutions as well as their attempt to adjust to their host society's cultural universe while maintaining their distinctive identity.

SEWA SINGH KALSI

List of Illustrations

A young Sikh boy wearing a turban and a ceremonial sword in the precinct of the Golden Temple, Amritsar

1 Founder
- NANAK DEV -

Guru Nanak Dev (centre) with the other nine human gurus and two attendants

Our quest for an understanding of the historical development of the Sikh tradition and an insight into Sikh culture must begin with a biographical sketch of its founder, Nanak Dev, popularly known as Guru Nanak, together with his reaction to the religious, social and political circumstances obtaining in fifteenth-century Punjab.

First, however, it is essential to decode the meaning of the word 'guru'. This takes us to the second stage: how the movement originated by Guru Nanak began to be known as Sikhism. *Sikh* means a student, a learner or a disciple, while the term *guru* denotes a teacher, an enlightener, or a spiritual guide. The terms 'guru' and 'sikh' (Punjabi form of the Sanskrit word *shishya*) are derived from the Sanskrit language.

The Sikh tradition, like most Indic-religious traditions, such as Hinduism, Buddhism and Jainism, is a guru-sikh (teacher-disciple)-oriented organization in which the relationship between a guru and his/her disciple is regarded as most sacred and distinct.

How a guru is perceived

A guru, whether a man or a woman, is perceived as the captain of a ship who guides his/her followers across the ocean of worldly temptations while, at the same time, paving the way for spiritual salvation. According to Guru Nanak, the guru is not meant to benefit the chosen few. He is meant for the whole of humanity. He shows the way to everyone without reference to birth, sex, caste, colour or creed.

During his lifetime Guru Nanak attracted large numbers of followers who became his disciples or Sikhs and who in turn revered Nanak as their guru. Quite simply, this is how the Sikh movement began. Sikhs were originally the inhabitants of the state of Punjab who embraced the teachings of Nanak and his nine successors, and who under their creative leadership and teachings emerged as a distinct Sikh/Punjabi community.

PUNJABI HERITAGE

Scholars of the history of India generally agree that it is one of the oldest civilizations in the world and that its cradle was the soil of Punjab. Its cities were known as Mohenjodaro and Harappa and scholars sometimes refer to it as the Indus Valley civilization. It dates back to between 7,000-20,000 BC.

Derivation of 'Punjab'

The most significant factor concerning the development of the Indus Valley civilization was undoubtedly its fertile soil and the five rivers (Jehlum, Chenab, Ravi, Sutlej and Beas) that provided a constant supply of water for irrigation. Interestingly, the term Punjab is comprised of two words: *Punj* meaning five and *ab* meaning water, thus the land of five rivers.

The arrival of the Aryan people from the west into the Punjab, around 1500 BC, had a dramatic impact on Punjabi society. The social interaction between the Aryans and the indigenous people resulted in a new culture which resulted in a caste system evolving in India. It was also in the Punjab that the Aryans evolved their Vedic culture and recorded the Vedas and other great works of the Sanskrit language.

The Aryans were followed by numerous invaders, including Greeks, Turks and Mughals, all of whom entered India through the Punjab and left their cultural mark on Punjabi identity. It is interesting to note that the Urdu language evolved and developed under the impact of social interaction between Persian soldiers and Punjabi people.

For our purposes the invasion of the Mughal emperor Babar is particularly significant. It is believed that Guru Nanak witnessed the slaughter of ordinary Punjabi people at the hands of the Islamic Mughal army at Aimnabad in 1526. Commenting upon the social and political degeneration of the society at that time, Nanak said: 'Kings are butchers: cruelty is their weapon. The sense of duty has taken wings and vanished. Falsehood reigns over the land as a veil of darkness.'

Ironically, Mughal rule in India contributes significantly towards the development of the Sikh tradition and its principle institutions. As a matter of fact, the Punjab and India enjoyed a relatively peaceful life under the Mughal rulers. The interaction between Hinduism and Islam had a major impact on the development of the Sikh tradition.

GURU NANAK

Guru Nanak was born into a Khatri family (one of the high castes in Hindu society) in 1469 in a village called Talwandi located about forty miles from the city of Lahore (now in Pakistan). His father was a revenue officer. Being the son of a government official, Nanak was privileged to be educated both in the Sanskrit and Persian languages by Hindu and Muslim teachers. From a very young age, he is believed to have had a craving for answers to the meaning and purpose of human existence. Thus he began to enjoy the company of wandering *Sadhus* and *Sants* (religious mendicants/hermits) and Sufi leaders of Islam. He was also deeply distressed, we are told, by the social divisions in Punjabi/Indic society which had been rationalized by the Hindu hierarchy as part of the divine order.

While working at Sultanpur as a manager of government stores, Nanak gained a personal insight into the way state structures functioned. Apparently, he was very disturbed by having to witness the moral degradation and degeneration of government officials who were engaged in the exploitation of ordinary people through a system of bribes and oppression.

Nanak, in fact, appeared at a critical period in the history of India when it was drifting fast into the hands of the Mughal invaders after the earlier invasions of Muslim rulers from Central Asia. Hindu society, dominated by the Brahmins (highest caste), was bitterly divided within numerous caste groups and steeped in ritualistic practices, whereas the Muslim hierarchy, encouraged by the state, was engaged in the process of converting the Hindu population.

Challenge to hypocrisy

Nanak subsequently strongly denounced the hypocrisy of the traditional Hindu leaders. He is recorded as saying: 'Look at the behaviour of the traditional Hindu leaders; they wear Islamic dress on duty and eat Muslim food but when they return home in the evening they change into their traditional Hindu dress, put a *tilak* (religious mark) on their forehead and smear the kitchen floor with cow-dung for ritual purification and then recite Vedic hymns while cooking vegetarian food.'

Nanak was a married man with two sons. He

challenged the attitude of Yogis and Sannyasis (a sect of renouncers) who advocated the practice of celibacy and renunciation of society for spiritual liberation. He preached that one must live amongst people and share their joys and disappointments, and be an agent of change for the eradication of outmoded rituals and superstitious practices.

DIVINE CALL

According to Sikh tradition, Nanak received the divine call at Sultanpur. One morning, when he went to bathe in the nearby river, it is believed that he was taken to God's court. He reappeared after three days declaring: 'There is no Hindu and there is no Muslim.' His declaration was focused on the unity and equality of humankind transcending the sectarian boundaries of caste and religious bigotry.

Key principle: The Oneness of God

Seen as a creative genius, Nanak did not merely denounce and condemn the caste system and morally-degrading customs and rituals. For him, the ultimate purpose of human existence was to comprehend the true meaning of the concept of the oneness of God by celebrating the diversity in God's kingdom.

He took practical steps to translate his ideas and set out on a long journey through India and abroad with a mission to visit various centres of learning. For his companion, he chose Mardana, a Muslim minstrel, in order to express his understanding of the oneness of God.

During his travels Nanak composed *bani* (writings) in poetic form in Punjabi, the language of ordinary people rather than Sanskrit or Persian. He thereby removed the barrier between God and people and released them from the clutches of religious zealots like the Brahmins. While Nanak composed poetry, Mardana set it to music and sang. Since then the tradition of *shabad-kirtan* (religious singing) has become an integral part of a Sikh service.

Accompanied by Mardana, the two of them are believed to have travelled to Mecca where Nanak imparted the message of the oneness of God to the custodians of Islam. He also visited the religious centres of the Hindus, Buddhists and Muslims in India. While in Mecca he was asked who was superior, a Hindu or a Muslim, to which he replied that without good deeds both were living in darkness. He proclaimed that 'Truth is high but higher still is truthful living'.

On one occasion, he visited Hardwar, one of the ancient Hindu centres of pilgrimage, situated on the banks of the river Ganges. He stood with the pilgrims in the river for an early morning bathe; they were praying while throwing water towards the rising sun. Nanak, however, began to throw water to the west. The people around him were surprised to see someone acting against the centuries-old Hindu tradition of offering water to their ancestors.

As a result, Nanak was brought before the custodians of Hardwar. They questioned his behaviour and asked what he had been doing in the river Ganges that morning. He replied that he was watering his fields in his village near Lahore. The Brahmins laughed at his explanation and replied: 'Your water could not reach the fields in the Punjab which are nearly two hundred miles away from Hardwar.' 'Then, how far is the sun and your ancestors from Hardwar?' asked Nanak. They replied that the sun was millions and millions of miles from earth. 'If my water cannot reach my fields a few hundred miles from Hardwar', responded Nanak, 'how can your water possibly reach your ancestors and the god Sun which is so far away from earth?' The Brahmins were speechless in the face of Nanak's question which had exposed the futility of one of their superstitious rituals.

□

After more than twenty years of extensive travel, Nanak returned to the Punjab and settled at Kartarpur (literally 'God's village/town'), a town he founded on the banks of the River Ravi. It was at Kartarpur that he began to give practical shape to his revolutionary ideas. He launched a crusade against the caste divisions. He despised the exclusion of low caste people from entering and worshipping at Hindu temples. Being a visionary leader, he innovated the traditions of *sangat* (communal worship) and *langar* (communal meal) for transmitting the message of God's oneness. He also preached the significance of *kirat-karna* (earning one's living through honest means) and *wand-chhakna* (sharing the fruits of one's labours with others.

At Kartarpur, Nanak's house was turned into a *dharamsala* (a place of worship) where people of different castes and faiths would gather for *shabad-kirtan* (religious singing) and a common meal while sitting in rows, without any distinction of gender or status. Kartarpur became a very popular centre and it began to be visited by large numbers of people who became Nanak's followers or 'Sikhs'.

During his travels, Nanak had collected the writings of Muslim and Hindu saints alike, some of whom were born in the lowest caste groups, for example, Kabir, Farid, Ravidas. Before his death in 1539, Nanak appointed Angad, one of his disciples, as his successor for continuing his mission, and gave him the collection of writings of other saints as well as his own compositions for the spiritual nurturing of future generations. His decision to choose his successor was one of the cardinal steps that laid the foundation of the institution of guruship in the Sikh tradition.

FUNDAMENTAL INSTITUTIONS OF SIKHISM

Nanak was followed by nine guru successors who further evolved and developed some of the fundamental institutions of Sikhism, for example, the Golden Temple (Harmandir Sahib), the Sikh scriptures (Adi Granth), the place of worship (gurdwara) and the Sikh brotherhood (Khalsa) which played a crucial role in bestowing a distinctive identity to the movement originated by him.

THE TEN GURUS

Guru Nanak	1469-1539	Guru Hargobind	1595-1644
Guru Angad	1504-1552	Guru Har Rai	1630-1661
Guru Amar Das	1479-1574	Guru Hari Krishan	1656-1664
Guru Ram Das	1534-1581	Guru Teg Bahadur	1621-1675
Guru Arjun Dev	1563-1606	Guru Gobind Singh	1666-1708

2 Teachings

Reading from the Sikh scriptures – the Guru Granth Sahib

ONENESS OF GOD

The central teaching in Sikhism is the belief in the concept of the oneness of God. All people, irrespective of caste, creed, colour and sex, are regarded as the creation of the one God. The notion of diversity in God's kingdom is perceived as a dynamic and positive force. It is believed that all religious traditions are equally valid and capable of enlightening their followers. By belonging to different traditions and standing in different places, all human beings can share and broaden one another's vision.

Sikhism rejects the view that any particular religion

has the monopoly concerning the absolute truth about God. According to Sikh teachings, all human groups evolved and developed their modes of worship and religious institutions within the context of their social environment. Whilst a Muslim prayer is called *namaz*, a Hindu prayer is *puja*, and a Sikh prayer is called *ardas*.

Universality of truth

The tenth Guru, Gobind Singh, highlighting the essence and universality of religious truth, wrote:

> Recognize all mankind, whether Muslim or Hindu as one.
> The same God is the Creator and Nourisher of all.
> Recognize no distinctions among them.
> The temple and mosque are the same.
> So are Hindu worship and Muslim prayer.
> Human beings are all one.

> (Dasam Granth 1078)

MUL-MANTRA

Guru Nanak's understanding of the nature of God is clearly depicted in his first composition popularly known as the *Mul-Mantra* (basic creed). The text and translation of the *Mul-Mantra* is given as follows:

Ek Onkar (There is One God)
Sat Nam (Eternal Truth is His name)
Karta Purkh (Creator of all things and the all pervading spirit)
Nirbhau (He is without fear)
Nirvair (He is without enmity)
Akal Murat (He is timeless and formless)

Ajuni (He is beyond birth and death)
Saibham (He is self-existent)
Gur parsad (He is known by the grace of the
   Guru)

Adi Granth I

The opening phrase, '*Ek Onkar*' summarizes the fundamental belief in Sikhism. The word *Ek* means one and *Onkar* denotes God, thus the emphasis is on the notion of the oneness of God. The Sikh scriptures begin with the *Mul-Mantra* which occurs more than a hundred times throughout the texts. It signifies the centrality of the belief in the concept of the oneness of God in Sikhism. Although the pronoun 'He' has been applied when referring to *Onkar* (God in English), in fact, in Sikhism God has no particular gender which further emphasizes the unity and equality of mankind.

MONOTHEISM

Guru Nanak preached strict monotheism. He disapproved of the worship of idols and the belief in the reincarnation of God. Since God is without any form, colour, mark or lineage, he cannot be established or installed as an idol. However, since God is infinite, He cannot die to be reincarnated nor could He assume human form as Hindus believe to be the case, who worship Lord Rama and Krishna as God in human form on earth.

The social and spiritual dimensions of the nature of God are intertwined in Sikh teaching. For example, if God is Truth, to speak an untruth is to be ungodly as untruthful conduct not only hurts one's fellow men it is also irreligious. Sikh gurus taught that a Sikh must not only believe in One, Omnipresent God, but also behave in such a way that he does not harm others by his hurtful conduct.

HUKAM – DIVINE ORDER

The term *hukam* came to the Punjabi vocabulary from the Arabic tradition; it means Divine Order. *Hukam* literally means order and *hakam* denotes the one who gives orders. The Sikh gurus applied the concept of *hukam* extensively in their compositions to explain the nature of creation, the universe and human life. According to the Sikh tradition, everything in this world functions according to the Divine Order or scheme. Guru Nanak, in his celebrated hymn called *Japji*, refers to the notion of *hukam* in order to demonstrate the hand of God behind the functioning of the universe as well as the daily life of human beings. Human life is understood to be part of the Divine Order, therefore it is man's duty to submit to God's Will. Expanding on the true meaning of the concept of *hukam*, Sikh gurus refer to the most important aspects of human existence, such as birth and death, which are beyond man's control.

Guru Nanak elaborates the notion of *hukam* by posing a question:

How may man purify himself?
How does man demolish the wall of ignorance?
This is brought about by living in accordance with God's Command or Will.

(Adi Granth 1)

Sikh teachings emphasize faith in the concept of *hukam*. It is stated that there is a Divine purpose in everything. Human beings cannot know the Divine mysteries; they are only a drop in the ocean or like a fish in the sea. It is therefore their duty to submit before God's Will. In their teachings, Sikh gurus have constantly reiterated that in the long run falsehood or evil will be destroyed and Truth will prevail. The martyrdom of the fifth guru, Arjun Dev as well as the ninth guru, Teg Bahadur, is perceived as *hukam* to which they submitted without complaining.

The doctrine of *hukam* raises a fundamental question: Are human beings helpless creatures in this world? No, said the gurus. They taught that all human beings have been endowed with qualities to create their own destiny. If a human being commits evil deeds he/she will suffer accordingly. It has been made absolutely clear that one reaps what one sows. It implies that for the attainment of Truth one needs to engage him/herself in righteous deeds.

DHARMSAL – PRACTICE OF RIGHTEOUSNESS

The term *dharmsal* is composed of two words: *dharm* which means religious, moral and social obligations while *sal* means a place of abode. Guru Nanak describes the earth as *dharmsal* (a place to practise righteousness) established by God within the universe, and human life as the highest form of God's kingdom; moreover, the earth and everything that stands on it carries the divine stamp. According to Sikh teachings, a Sikh is not a passive spectator in this world; he/she is expected to be an active participant in the drama of human affairs. The concept of *dharmsal* implies faith in the oneness of God and the equality of humankind. Thus, for a Sikh, there is no place for the renunciation of society and the pursuit of God in the forest abdicating all social responsibilities.

AWAGAUN – CYCLE OF BIRTH AND DEATH

The concept of *awagaun* denotes the belief in the cycle of birth and death. The Sikhs believe in the cycle of birth and death that depends upon one's conduct in this world. The concept of *awagaun* is based on the traditional belief in the doctrine of *karma* and the transmigration of the soul. It is believed that there are 8,400,000 lives (*chaurasi lakh joon*) before one is reborn as a human being. The soul is regarded as immortal; it passes from one form of life to another depending upon one's deeds (*karma*) done in this world. Those who are sinful and engage themselves in evil-doing keep going through the cycle of birth and death which is regarded as the most degrading state.

In order to overcome the ultimate punishment of going through the cycle of birth and death, a Sikh is required to conduct him/herself according to the teachings of the Sikh gurus. It means that he/she must work towards attaining the status of a *gursikh* (guru-oriented) as opposed to *manmukh* (self-oriented) 'person'. He/she is taught to lead a life of an honest householder, a true believer in the oneness of God and equality of humankind while earning a living by honest means and sharing it with others. At a Sikh funeral, the *granthi* (religious functionary) recites the *antam-ardas* (last prayer) invoking God's forgiveness for the departed soul and saving him/her from *awagaun*.

Sikhism rejects the traditional Hindu view that one's low caste status is the result of bad deeds in the previous life. According to Sikh teachings, human life is the most precious of all forms of life, and it is a gift of God. In this life we are offered the opportunity of engaging ourselves in righteous deeds in order to transcend the bonds of birth and death, and attain spiritual liberation (*mukti*). Those who follow the gurus' teachings and conduct themselves accordingly achieve the status of a *jiwan-mukta* (one who has conquered the worldly temptations and cut across the cycle of birth and death). The death of a *jiwan-mukta* is perceived as a gradual transition from earthly existence to existence in heaven.

MUKTI – SPIRITUAL LIBERATION

The word *mukti* is the Punjabi version of the Sanskrit term *moksha* which means 'to be free from', 'to release' or 'to liberate'. As a religious concept, it means the final release or spiritual liberation of the soul from human existence, leading to its merger with the Supreme Soul of *Parmatma* (God). The term *Parmatma* is composed of two words: *parm* meaning supreme and *atma* meaning soul. In Sikhism, the concept of *mukti* is applied to working towards spiritual release from the bondage of life and death. The attainment of *mukti* depends upon the conduct of human beings in this world.

In order to attain the status of a *gur-mukh* (guru-oriented person), a Sikh must endeavour to engage him/herself in righteous deeds. By conquering worldly temptations or evils, e.g. *kam* (lust), *karodh* (anger), *lobh* (greed), *moh* (attachment), *ahankar* (ego, pride), a Sikh rejects the life-style of a *man-mukh* (self-oriented) and becomes a *jiwan-mukta* while leading a life of detachment and dispassion. He/she is like a lotus which remains clean despite living in muddy water.

GURPARSAD – GRACE & BLESSINGS

The term *gurparsad* is composed of two words: *gur/guru* and *parsad*. The word *parsad* is derived from the Sanskrit language; it means grace, blessing and boon. It is the last word in the *Mul-mantra*. Here the word (gur/guru) does not stand for any personal *guru* but for the Eternal Guru or God. Thus the term *gurparsad* means realizing God by the guru's grace.

Several terms have been used by the Sikh gurus for elaborating the essence of the concept of *gurparsad/* grace, e.g. *karam*, *mehar* and *kirpa*. The word *karam* is derived from the Arabic language; *mehar* is from the Persian while *kirpa* comes from the Sanskrit.

3 Sikh Traditions

Initiated Sikh woman preparing *karah-parshad* (ritual food)

THE CASTE SYSTEM

Nanak and his successors were operating in a caste-ridden Hindu society in which individual status was ascribed on the basis of one's birth into a particular caste. There was no meaningful social intercourse between members of different caste groups. The caste status was closely linked to one's traditional occupation and it was also the symbol of caste identity within society. For example, the son of a carpenter inherited his traditional occupation as well as his caste identity from his parents. Moreover, it was his caste *dharma* to marry within his own caste group. Each caste group had its caste council (*panchayat*) which was responsible for enforcing caste *dharma*. This is how the boundaries of the caste system were clearly marked and defended.

Sikh gurus were acutely aware of the destructive impact of the caste system on the social, religious and cultural fabric of Indian society. They vehemently rejected the Hindu doctrine of *varnashramadharma* (laws of social classes/castes and stages of life) which they held to be based on caste exclusiveness and institutionalized inequality.

According to the ideology of the *varnashramadharma*/caste system, Hindu society is divided into four caste groups: Brahmins, Kshatriyas, Vaishyas and Shudras. The Shudras are further divided into two groups: clean and unclean. Unclean Shudras are also known as untouchables who live in their separate colonies known as *chamardlees* (literally the colony of chamars/leather workers).

These caste groups are organized hierarchically. The first three groups are called 'twice born' because only the men of these high caste groups are entitled to the initiation ceremony and wearing the sacred thread. Moreover, only 'twice born' males were entitled to hear the Vedas (Hindu scriptures). Thus both the Shudras and Hindu women were excluded from the privilege of the initiation ceremony and wearing sacred thread. Guru Nanak took the opposite view and condemned the differential treatment of Hindu women, preaching instead the equality of the sexes. He declared: 'How can we call her polluted from whom the noblest of the world are born?' (Adi Granth 473). In the hymn of *Jap Ji*, Nanak calls the earth '*mata dhart mahat* (The Great Earth is Mother of all). (Adi Granth 9).

Rejecting the falsehood of caste status, Nanak wrote:

phakar jati phakar nau, sabna jia ika chhau
(Worthless is caste and worthless an exalted name.
(For all mankind there is but only one refuge).
(Adi Granth 83)

Nanak and his successors did not merely condemn and denounce the caste system but took some practical steps to eradicate social divisions within Hindu society. Nanak strongly rejected the exclusionary practices enforced by the Hindu hierarchy and regarded such practices as a hindrance in understanding the true meaning of the concept of the oneness of God.

Nanak's challenge to the caste system stems from his own interpretation of the notion of *dharma*. He defines *dharma* as a mystical bull of Indian mythology which is believed to support and carry the entire earth on its horns.

What is Dharma?

Reflecting on the concept of *dharma* in Sikh tradition, Taran Singh says: '*Dharma* is that behaviour or conduct of man which supports and sustains total life, e.g. moral, physical, social and spiritual.'

Nanak's understanding of *dharma*, therefore, is based on universalism which is entirely contrary to the traditional Hindu view in which men follow their own *dharma* according to their social class/caste or stage of life.

Nanak innovated some of the fundamental institutions that have now become an integral part of the Sikh tradition. Let us now take a closer look at the nature and impact of these innovations upon the emergence and development of a new entity called Sikh Dharma in Punjabi and Sikhism in English.

□

SANGAT – COMMUNAL WORSHIP/SIKH CONGREGATION

The term *sangat* denotes the company of saintly persons. Nowadays, it is mainly used to describe the congregation at a gurdwara. According to Sikh tradition, Guru Nanak would invite all people, irrespective of caste, creed and gender, for religious singing and collective worship at his residence. They all had to sit in the same room rubbing shoulders with members of high and low caste groups. Perhaps, it was the first time in their life when they really felt that they were members of one human family. The institution of *sangat* has emerged as one of the most powerful and democratic institutions within Sikh society.

In the early period of the Sikh movement, an assembly of devotees in the presence of Sikh gurus constituted a *sangat*. Sikh gurus also appointed their nominees called *masand* to supervise the newly-emerging *sangats* all over the country. Members of the Sikh congregation participating in the service automatically constitute a *sangat*. The *sangat* is empowered to take decisions concerning the general welfare of the Sikh community. A resolution approved by the *sangat* is called *gurmata* (literally guru's intention) which is unreservedly followed by members of the congregation.

The Adi Granth – Guru Granth Sahib

The tenth guru, Gobind Singh, terminated the line of human gurus and transferred his personal authority to the Adi Granth before his death in 1708. Since then the Adi Granth is known as the Guru Granth Sahib. The instalment of the Guru Granth Sahib is mandatory at a Sikh service.

There are no formal qualifications for membership of a *sangat*. Any Sikh, irrespective of caste and gender, present at a Sikh congregation is regarded as a member of the *sangat*. The *sangat* is distinctly an autonomous institution. However, the day-to-day management of the community-based gurdwaras is conducted by the management committees which are organized according to the constitutions of the respective gurdwaras.

The *sangat* is a gurdwara's main source of financial support. Members of the *sangat* make generous donations towards the running expenses of gurdwaras including Punjabi classes for Sikh children. They also collect funds for supporting medical and educational projects in India and victims of floods and earthquakes etc.

The *sangat* plays a crucial role in the spiritual nurturing of Sikh generations. Sikh children accompany their parents to the gurdwara from a very young age. They learn the rules of Sikh behaviour by imitating their parents and other members of the *sangat*. Children's belief in the diversity and equality of humankind gets confirmed as soon as they join the *sangat*. They begin to understand the equality of the sexes when their parents sit on the same carpet alongside other members of the congregation. Children also observe women reading the Adi Granth (Sikh scriptures) and taking part in *shabad-kirtan* (religious singing).

The terminology for the *sangat* applied by Sikh preachers and other religious functionaries provides some insight into the perceived status of this institution. For example, the most popular phrases applied by them are: '*guru di pyari sadh-sangat* (guru's beloved saintly congregation) or *guru roop sad-sangat* (guru's true self-saintly congregation). Here the status of a *sangat* is equated with that of the guru. In fact, the institution of the *sangat* is the backbone of every thriving Sikh community. The fourth guru, Ram Das, says: '*Sat sangat* is the school of the True Guru where a Sikh gets training in godly qualities' (AD 1316).

LANGAR – COMMUNAL MEAL

Langar is one of the cardinal Sikh institutions which reinforces the central message of the oneness of God. The institution of *langar* further confirms the notion of the equality of humankind already established by the institution of *sangat*. The term *langar* is derived from the Persian language which literally means 'anchor'. It applies both to the communal meal and the dining-room-cum-community kitchen where it is prepared and served to the people. It is respectfully called *guru ka langar* (literally food provided by the guru).

The term *guru ka langar* signifies the sanctity of food cooked and shared at a gurdwara. No Sikh will leave a gurdwara without taking *langar* in the dining hall. A visit to a gurdwara is perceived as *adhoory* (incomplete) if a Sikh is not able to join in sharing the communal meal. As a matter of fact, it has become second nature for Sikhs to eat *langar* after the conclusion of a service.

As mentioned earlier, the Sikh gurus launched a crusade against the caste system which perpetuated the caste distinctions and the notion of ritual purity and pollution. Members of high caste groups would not sit and dine with members of low caste groups. It was Nanak who innovated the institutions of *langar* and *sangat* to challenge the centuries-old tradition of caste divisions within Hindu society.

□

Traditionally, the food cooked at a gurdwara used to be very simple and strictly vegetarian. It would include *chapatees* (unleaven wheat bread cooked on a flat iron plate; it is called *roti* in Punjabi) and a *dal* (a mixture of black-eyed beans and split chick peas). The food is usually provided by the gurdwara. To mark some special occasions such as birthdays and marriages most Sikh families contribute and cook the whole *langar*; it is regarded as God's grace.

A group of Sikh pilgrims having *langar* (communal meal) in the traditional manner in the dining hall at Amritsar

A group of Sikh ladies preparing *langar*

The preparation of *langar* is undertaken by a team of volunteers. Both men and women enthusiastically participate in the preparation and distribution of food. During the preparation they would recite *shabads* (hymns) which signifies the special status accorded to the food popularly called *guru ka langar*. As soon as the food is ready, a portion is placed before the Adi Granth in the congregation hall. Now a *granthi* (reader of the Adi Granth) recites *ardas* (Sikh prayers) invoking God for blessings on the *langar*. After the *ardas*, the sanctified portion of food is mixed with the whole *langar* and served to the people.

The institution of *langar* has emerged as a powerful instrument for the eradication of caste divisions. It is also a bold statement in the belief in social equality. It played a paramount role in instilling the sense of community among the Sikhs. By the time of the third Guru, Amar Das, the institution of *langar* had attained a unique status within the rapidly growing Sikh community. Guru Amar Das made it mandatory for everyone to eat *langar* before going for his *darshan* (literally sight or view). According to Khushwant Singh: Guru Amar Das made the *langar* an integral institution of the Sikh church by insisting that anyone who wanted to see him had first to accept his hospitality by eating with the disciples.

It is recorded that Emperor Akbar ate *langar* before meeting Guru Amar Das. He was so impressed with the institution of *langar* that he donated several hundred acres of land to the guru. Royal patronage enormously enhanced the status of Guru Amar Das and provided further momentum to the rapidly developing Sikh movement.

PANGAT – SITTING TOGETHER

The institutions of *langar* and *pangat* are two inseparable parts of one tradition. *Pangat* literally means people sitting together in a row for a communal meal irrespective of caste, creed or status. *Pangat* signifies Nanak's resolve to demolish social barriers by educating people in understanding the message of the oneness of God through example. According to Sikh tradition, Guru Nanak used to sit with the *sangat* to eat his meals in the dining-room.

SEWA – VOLUNTARY SERVICE

Sewa literally means voluntary/selfless service performed for the community. The institutions of *sangat* and *langar* made enormous contributions towards the growth of the Sikh community. They emerged as two integrated constituents of gurdwara activities. Moreover, the institutions of *sangat* and *langar* promoted the sense of social responsibility among Sikhs. Most members of the *sangat* learn their initial lessons of *sewa* by working in the community kitchen. They would cook food, clean utensils, serve food and clean the kitchen and the dining hall. All such activities are undertaken by the *sewadars* (volunteers) who feel highly privileged to be able to perform *sewa* in the *langar*.

Most Sikh parents encourage their young children to do *sewa* at the gurdwara. They serve food in the dining hall and sometimes look after the shoes of the *sangat*. Sikh volunteers clean and prepare the main congregation hall every week. Until the mid 1970s all religious functionaries at the gurdwaras in Britain used to be *sewadars*. Selfless or voluntary service (*sewa*) is one of the cardinal principles of Sikh conduct. The concept of *sewa* is closely linked with the notion of *dharmsal* propounded by Guru Nanak who taught his followers to engage themselves in righteous deeds by serving the community. Bhai Gurdas, scribe of the Adi Granth, emphasized the significance of voluntary service and sharing food:

> The Sikhs should serve one another;
> Only by serving others, one can attain happiness,
> One should cultivate selfless devotion and share one's food with others.
>
> (Bhai Gurdas Var 20, pauri 10)

The establishment of gurdwaras is regarded as true *sewa* by Sikhs. The *kar sewa* (voluntary service for clearing the silt from the reservoir of the Golden Temple) is regarded by Sikhs as one of the most auspicious projects for doing *sewa*. The holy reservoir is cleaned at regular intervals. Sikhs throughout the world are informed about this most momentous event.

The significance of *sewa* was emphasized by Guru Nanak who wrote: 'A place in God's court can only be attained if we do service to others in this world.' (AG 26) He also warned that 'Wandering ascetics, warriors, celibates, sannyasis, none of them obtains fruit (spiritual liberation) without performing *sewa*' (AG 992).

The spirit of *sewa* was one of the key factors in creating a new social and religious awakening amongst the Sikhs.

KIRAT KARNA – EARNING ONE'S LIVING BY WORKING

Kirat literally means work and *karna* denotes 'to do'. The phrase *kirat karna* represents one of the cardinal rules of Sikh behaviour. It has contributed towards forging social awareness amongst the Sikhs. Nanak was highly critical of those who lived on other people's earnings and exploited them for their own selfish gratification. He declared that 'Encroachment upon what rightfully belongs to others is forbidden to both Muslims and Hindus, as pork to the former and beef to the latter' (AD 141).

At Kartarpur, Nanak took to agriculture for living and set an example for transmitting the message of *kirat karna*. He denounced the behaviour of *jogis* (renunciates) who after renouncing society begged food from householders.

The episode of Bhai Lalo and Malik Bhago is very popular amongst the Sikhs; it signifies the importance of *kirat karna* for them. According to Sikh tradition, Guru Nanak stayed with Bhai Lalo at Aimnabad during his travels. Bhai Lalo was a carpenter and a Shudra by caste. Malik Bhago, the landlord of the village, and other high caste people disapproved of the choice of residence by Guru Nanak. One day, Malik Bhago invited Nanak for a meal which he refused to accept. Nanak told Malik Bhago that his food was obtained by exploiting others while the food of Bhai Lalo had been earned by hard labour.

WAND CHHAKNA – SHARING ONE'S EARNINGS

The word *wand* means sharing and *chhakna* denotes eating. The phrase *wand chhakna* like *kirat karna* signifies another important rule of Sikh behaviour that has contributed enormously towards generating social awareness amongst Sikhs. Guru Nanak preached the principles of *kirat karna* and *wand chhakna* for the social, moral and spiritual development of his followers. He wrote: 'Only he who earns his living by the sweat of his brow and shares his earnings with others has discovered the path of righteousness, O, Nanak' (Var Sarang 1).

DASWANDH – DONATING ONE TENTH OF ONE'S EARNINGS TO THE GURU

The term *daswandh* is comprised of two words: *das* meaning ten and *wandh* which denotes a share. It is generally accepted that the collection of *daswandh* was introduced by the fifth guru, Arjun Dev, for raising funds for the building of the Golden Temple and other community projects. By his time the Sikh movement had spread widely and it had attracted a significant number of followers from all over the Punjab.

The institution of *masand* (guru's appointees), started by the third guru, Amar Das, had been especially instrumental in attracting new followers to the Sikh movement. Guru Arjun instructed his *masands* to collect *daswandh* from the Sikhs and bring it to Amritsar on the occasion of the Baisakhi festival (first day of the month of Baisakh in the Punjabi calendar).

In this way a central finance pool was created for the construction of the temple as well as for building other communal projects.

The collection of *daswandh* in its original form has become redundant. Nowadays, Sikhs make a free-will donation to a gurdwara on every visit. They also make generous donations to the historical gurdwaras, e.g. the Golden Temple and Gurdwara Sis Ganj in Delhi. The establishment of gurdwaras in the Sikh diaspora has been financed by the local Sikh communities, and such donations are regarded as *daswandh*. Interestingly, the tradition of collecting *daswandh* is very popular amongst the Namdhari Sikhs who believe in the continuity of the line of living gurus.

4 **Scriptures**

The *palki* (palanquin) inside a gurdwara which contains the scriptures

THE *ADI GRANTH*

The principal Sikh scriptures are contained in what is called the *Adi Granth* (p.33). It was compiled by the fifth guru, Arjun Dev, who completed the work in 1604. Its origin and development is closely linked with the process of the emergence and maturity of the Sikh tradition. The etymology (derivation) of the title of this unique document provides deep insight into the central teachings in Sikhism, for example, the concept of the oneness of God. The word *Adi* is derived from the Sanskrit meaning 'original' or 'eternal' and the word *Granth* denotes a book or a collection of compositions in a book form.

The word *Adi* is also linked with Nanak's most celebrated hymn *'Japji'* which begins with the statement that God is *Adi Sach* (true from the beginning) (AG 1). Thus the title Adi Granth conveys the belief that it had its origin in eternity. The notion of eternity refers to the *bani* (compositions in the Adi Granth). Addressing Bhai Lalo at Aimnabad, Guru Nanak said:

'Whatever Word I receive from the Lord,
I pass it on in the same strain, O, Lalo' (AD 722/23)

In this chapter, we shall look at the process of the compilation of the Adi Granth and how it was transformed from Adi Granth to the Guru Granth Sahib (pages 48/50) which, in fact, signifies the pivotal role of the institution of guruship in Sikh tradition.

The origin of the Adi Granth can be traced to Nanak's first utterance 'There is no Hindu and there is no Muslim' and his first composition which is popularly known as the *Mul-Mantra*. The multi-faith environment in which the Sikh tradition emerged and matured created unique opportunities for experiencing the true meaning of belonging to one human family. The Adi Granth contains the compositions of Sikh gurus alongside the writings of Muslim and Hindu saints, some of whom were born into the lowest strata of Indian society, e.g. Kabir, Frid and Ravidas.

HISTORICAL CONTEXT

The compilation of the Adi Granth began during the period of Nanak's extensive travels. Alongside his own compositions, Nanak collected and recorded the *bani* (writings) of Muslim and Hindu saints in a book called *pothi* (volume). Hindu and Muslim contributors to the Adi Granth composed their songs over a period of six centuries before Nanak's arrival. According to Sikh tradition, Nanak passed on his *pothi*/notebook to his successor, Angad Dev, at the time of his investiture as the second guru. Thereafter, Angad Dev prepared a number of copies of Nanak's *pothi* for the use at Sikh *sangats* in other centres. Before his death, Angad Dev handed over Nanak's *pothi* along with his own compositions to his successor, Amar Das.

Amar Das was a competent organizer. By this time the Sikh movement had expanded to many more localities in the Punjab. In order to cater for the needs of a rapidly growing Sikh community he introduced the system of *manjis* (seat of authority) and appointed his representatives called *masands* to organize worship and the collection of offerings. He had made more copies of the hymns of Nanak and Angad Dev and added to them his own compositions.

Before his death, Amar Das appointed Ram Das who was his son-in-law as his successor.

The fourth guru, Ram Das, also composed *bani* (compositions) like his predecessors. His youngest son, Arjun Dev, succeeded him as the fifth guru. He was a gifted poet and organizer. He also composed *bani* following the tradition of his predecessors. It was Guru Arjun who decided to bring together all the writings into a single volume for the benefit of the entire Sikh community. He secured the writings of his maternal grandfather, Amar Das, and added those of his father as well as his own, and called it the Adi Granth.

The momentous task of compiling the Adi Granth and the construction of the Golden Temple began simultaneously. The final version of the Adi Granth was completed in 1604.

After the compilation of the Adi Granth, Arjun Dev installed it in the Golden Temple and appointed Bhai Buddha, a Jat Sikh, as the first *granthi* (reader or custodian of the Adi Granth). This appointment challenged the role of Brahmin priests who for centuries had had control over the teaching of Hindu scriptures.

The original copy of the Adi Granth is called *Kartarpur Vali Bir* (literally Adi Granth of Kartarpur). Kartarpur is a town founded by the fifth guru, Arjun Dev; it is situated in the district of Jullundar. According to Sikh tradition, the sixth guru, Hargobind, moved to live in Kartarpur and he took the Adi Granth with him. The Adi Granth remained with the descendants of Dhir Mal (brother of the seventh guru, Har Rai) through the remainder of the seventeenth and the whole of the eighteenth centuries.

In 1849, the British army captured Lahore and found the Adi Granth in the Lahore Court. It was handed back to Sodhi Sadhu Singh of Kartarpur when he petitioned the British authorities in the Punjab for its return. Sodi Sadhu Singh prepared a copy of the Adi Granth and presented it to Queen Victoria as a mark of gratitude. This volume is now in the India Office and Records Library. Since then the original copy of the Adi Granth has remained in the possession of the Sodhi family at Kartarpur. On major festivals, the Sodhis display the Adi Granth for the benefit of pilgrims who make generous offerings to the scriptures.

FROM THE ADI GRANTH TO THE GURU GRANTH SAHIB

The transition from human guruship to that of the guruship invested in the Adi Granth was a slow process. It is believed that the tenth guru, Gobind Singh, prepared the final version by adding various writings by his father, the ninth guru, Teg Bahadur. It was completed in 1706 at the village of Talwandi Sabo, today known as Dam Dama Sahib. Thus, the final version of the Adi Granth is popularly known as the *Dam Dama Vali Bir*. It is acknowledged as the authorized version.

Guru Granth Sahib

Tradition records how the tenth Guru, Gobind Singh, terminated the line of human gurus by bestowing guruship on the Adi Granth. The ceremony of the transfer of personal authority to the Adi Granth is believed to have taken place before his death in 1708 at Nander/Hazoor Sahib in Maharashtra State, India. Since that moment the Adi Granth has been revered as a human guru, and is respectfully addressed as the Guru Granth Sahib.

The word Sahib means lord; it signifies the highest authority accorded by Sikhs to the Adi Granth. Accordingly, the Adi Granth is always positioned at a higher level than the *sangat* which is on floor level.

A Sikh waving a *chauri* (ritual fan) over the Adi Granth

Before the culmination of a service, the Adi Granth is opened by the *granthi* at random and the first hymn on the left-hand page is read out to the *sangat*; the reading is called *hukamnama* (guru's order for the day). The *hukamnama* signifies the culmination of the service with the authority of the guru as personified by the Adi Granth. The tradition of *hukamnama* has been inherited from the Sikh gurus who used to issue *hukamnamas* to the Sikhs during their ministry.

LANGUAGE OF THE ADI GRANTH

The Adi Granth is written in the *gurmukhi* (literally from the guru's mouth) script. Although the innovation of the *gurmukhi* script is attributed to the second guru, Angad Dev, there is diversity of opinion about the origin and antiquity of the Punjabi language and the *gurmukhi* script. However, it is generally accepted that the language of the Adi Granth is Punjabi. In fact, the largest portion of the scriptures is written in Sant Bhasha or Hindvi which is a mixture of Hindi, Parakrit, Braj and Punjabi. Like the notion of religious diversity, Sikh gurus skilfully employed and celebrated linguistic diversity for reinforcing the deep meanings of the oneness of God.

STRUCTURE OF THE ADI GRANTH

The current volume of the Adi Granth has 1430 pages. It contains 5894 hymns (*shabads* and *shalokas*). The total number of hymns attributed to each contributor is as follows:

Guru Nanak Dev: 974

Guru Angad Dev:	62
Guru Amar Das:	907
Guru Ram Das:	679
Guru Arjun Dev:	2,218
Guru Teg Bahadur:	116

The main Hindu and Muslim contributors are:

Kabir:	541
Farid:	116
Namdev:	60
Ravi Das:	41

Source: Cole and Sambhi 1978:189

The Adi Granth is arranged according to a musical setting (*ragas*) in which each hymn is meant to be sung. It was Nanak who innovated the tradition of *shabad-kirtan* that has become an integral part of the Sikh service everywhere. A relay of religious musicians at the Golden Temple continuously perform *shabad-kirtan* for twenty-one hours a day which confirms the pivotal role of the *shabad-kirtan* within the Sikh tradition.

CENTRALITY OF THE ADI GRANTH

Let us now take a brief look at the history of the process of seeking guidance from a living guru to that of the Adi Granth/Guru Granth Sahib. The change was not only painful for the Sikhs who were used to seeking guidance from the living guru but was fraught with unexpected difficulties. Many Sikhs refused to accept the authenticity of the episode of bestowing guruship to the Adi Granth by the tenth Guru, Gobind Singh. The Namdhari Sikhs, for example, (Ch. 9) do not believe in the death of Gobind Singh at Nander in 1708 and the transfer of his personal power to the Adi Granth.

At this point, we need to review the reasons for the confusion within the Sikh movement before and after the death of Gobind Singh. With the death of Gobind Singh, who was forced to evacuate Anandpur by the Mughal army, the Sikhs had also lost the control of their central headquarters. Moreover, the control of the Golden Temple had already passed into the hands of the descendants of Pirthi Chand, elder brother of Guru Arjun, since the period of the sixth guru, Hargobind. Guru Hargobind had established his headquarters at Kiratpur a town founded by him in the foothills of the Himalayas in 1634. The absence of the guru from the main centres of activity such as Amritsar, Goindwal and Anandpur affected the development of the Sikh movement; it also strengthened the hands of the guru's rivals within the guru household.

The appointment of Teg Bahadur as the ninth Guru and the legitimate successor of the eighth Guru was by no means a peaceful transition. Tradition records that when Teg Bahadur, after his investiture, went to pay his homage at the Golden Temple, the custodians of the temple slammed the doors in his face. As a result, he was forced to establish his headquarters at Anandpur. At that time, the Sikh movement was suffering from internal divisions as well as the Mughal policy of repression. After 1644, Teg Bahadur never again set foot in Amritsar, nor did his successor, the tenth guru Gobind in the Punjab.

During this period the importance of Amritsar as the

central headquarters had seriously weakened. Following the death of Gobind Singh, the Sikh community found itself confronted with the dilemma of the absence of the living Guru on the one hand and the loss of their central headquarters on the other.

Ironically, the disintegration of the Mughal empire began with the death of Emperor Aurangzeb in 1707. At that time Gobind Singh was staying at Nander, suffering from a fatal wound. Analysing the political situation, he chose the charismatic Banda Bahadur to lead the Punjabi Sikhs and issued *hukamnamas*, urging them to join forces with Banda Bahadur.

With the support of the Punjabi Sikhs, he established the first sovereign Sikh state in 1710, and issued new coins bearing the names of Guru Nanak and Guru Gobind Singh to mark the establishment of the new state. Khushwant Singh says: 'His [Banda Bahadur] seal had inscribed on it not only the names of the gurus but also the two things which had contributed most to the popularity and power of the Sikhs and their church – the *degh* or cauldron in the guru's *langar* and *tegh*, the sword of the Khalsa.'

Although Banda's rule over the newly-established Sikh/Punjabi state came to an end with his arrest and execution in 1716, he had ushered in a wave of political awakening amongst the Punjabi people. His execution was watched by thousands of citizens, including two Englishmen who were then in attendance at the Mughul court in Delhi.

After the death of Banda Bahadur, the Sikhs became divided into two factions. One group called themselves Bandai (followers of Banda Bahadur) who revered him as a guru while the others called themselves members of the Tat Khalsa (pure Khalsa who believed in the termination of the line of human gurus after the tenth guru, Gobind Singh). Commenting on the internal divisions among the Sikhs, Madanjit Kaur writes: '. . . The Bandais had already made themselves distinct by adopting a different garb and by refusing to accept the authority of Guru Granth as the Guru of the Sikhs.'

Now both factions were struggling to gain control over the Golden Temple in order to establish their authority over the Sikhs' central shrine. At one stage both factions were ready to use physical force when Mani Singh, the custodian of the Golden Temple, intervened. The dispute was settled by casting lots. Two pieces of paper carrying the names of the factions, were floated in the Holy Tank [reservoir around the Golden Temple] at the place known as Har Ki Pauri. The piece of paper bearing the name of the Tat Khalsa (Fateh waheguru ji ki) kept floating while the other sank. So the decision was given in favour of Tat Khalsa. The significance of this episode lies in the fact that the authority of the Guru Granth Sahib as the guru of the Sikhs remained a contentious issue for a considerable time after the death of Guru Gobind Singh.

After the Death of Banda Bahadur the Sikh movement came under serious attack by the Moghul authorities. By 1765 the Sikhs had organized themselves into twelve *misls* (armies) each operating under an independent leader. They used to meet and celebrate the festival of Diwali (festival of lights) at the Golden Temple every year. These meetings were popularly known as the '*Sarbat Khalsa*' (literally the meeting of the whole Sikh community). We are now witnessing the emergence of two unique institutions within the Sikh movement: *gurmata* and the Sarbat Khalsa. These two institutions were highly instrumental in promoting the concept of the Adi Granth as the Guru Granth Sahib within the Sikh movement.

In 1799 Maharaja Ranjit Singh, leader of one of the Sikh *misls*, captured Lahore and laid the foundation of an independent Sikh/Punjabi state in the Punjab. Ranjit Singh disbanded the *misls* and emerged as a sovereign ruler of the Punjab. With the disbanding of the Sikh *misls* the institution of the Sarbat Khalsa lost its authority. In 1849 the British forces annexed the Punjab and took control of the Sikh shrines as well. The Deputy Commissioner of Amritsar was entrusted with the control of the Golden Temple by order of the Governor-General, who appointed a committee of Sikh landlords to assist him with the management of the temple.

The rise of Singh Sabha, a Sikh reform movement founded in 1873 in Amritsar, was a key factor in promoting the authority of the Adi Granth as the Guru of the Sikh community. The Sikh reformers skilfully used the printing press for producing copies of the Adi Granth with a standard text. They also revived the institution of *gurmata* and challenged the authority of *masands* (traditional custodians of the historical gurdwaras) who had grabbed control for their personal gratification.

Nowadays, Sikhs respect the Guru Granth Sahib very highly, like their ten gurus, but do not worship it. The presence of the Guru Granth Sahib is regarded as mandatory on almost all ceremonial and domestic occasions, i.e. wedding, initiation ceremony, naming ceremony, and processions taken out on the anniversaries of Sikh gurus etc.

THE DASAM GRANTH

The second scriptural book of the Sikhs is called the Dasam Granth or Dasven Padshah Ka Granth 'The Granth of the Tenth Guru'. The tenth guru, Gobind Singh was a poetic genius who, it is believed, composed poetry on many topics. He had fifty-two bards in his court at Anandpur. Tradition recalls how most of his writings and the work of the bards were lost at the time of their exit from Anandpur under severe pressure from the Mughul army. It is believed that Bhai Mani Singh, one of the trusted disciples of Gobind Singh, spent nine years collecting and reproducing the guru's works. His task was completed in 1734 at Amritsar, and Bhai Mani Singh named it 'Dasven Padshah ka Granth'.

There were other copies of the collection attributed to Gobind Singh besides the one compiled by Mani Singh. In 1885, the Singh Sabha appointed a committee of scholars to resolve the issue of the scriptures' authenticity. In 1902, the committee published an authorized version, giving it the name 'Dasam Granth' for the first time. This version of the Dasam Granth is in general circulation and comprises 1,428 pages.

☐

Most of the Dasam Granth is in Braj – a mixture of Sanskrit and Hindi – and is written in *gurmukhi* script. Two compositions are in Persian, one of which is called *Zafar Nama*, a long letter written to the Mughul emperor Aurangzeb by Gobind Singh. Another long composition attributed to Gobind Singh is *Bachitar Natak* (literally Wondrous Drama); it is believed to be the autobiography of the tenth Guru. The Dasam Granth also contains several hymns which are in Punjabi, and are very popular amongst Sikhs and are enthusiastically recited and sung at the Baisakhi festival as well as at the birth celebrations of Guru Gobind Singh.

☐

Following the compilation of the Dasam Granth, Sikhs paid the same reverence to it as to the Adi Granth. In actual fact, both scriptures used to be present at the meetings of the Sarbat Khalsa and both received the same reverence.

With the rise of radical elements in the Singh Sabha movement, the situation gradually changed. The Sikh reformers concentrated on the supremacy of the Adi Granth, relying on two factors in particular. Firstly, because it was the Adi Granth which was installed in the Golden Temple by the fifth guru, Arjun Dev, and secondly because the tenth guru Gobind Singh bestowed guruship on the Adi Granth while at the same time terminating the line of human gurus and requiring Sikhs to revere Adi Granth as a living guru after his death. Although the Dasam Granth is not installed in the gurdwaras, some of its compositions such as *Jap, Swayyas, Shabad Hazarey, Chaupai* are recited during the preparation of *amrit* (water of immortality prepared for the initiation ceremony) and other acts of worship.

5 The Gurdwara & Sikh Worship

View of the Golden Temple at Amritsar

The gurdwara has emerged as one of the central institutions in the Sikh tradition. The term gurdwara comprises two words: 'Guru' and 'dwara'. 'Dwara' means 'house or the doorway'; 'guru' denotes scripture or the Guru Granth Sahib. The gurdwara is the main centre of Sikh worship as well as the focus for the social and moral nurturing of those following the Sikh tradition. It is inconceivable to think of a Sikh community without a gurdwara. Its origin can be traced back to the founder Guru Nanak.

According to tradition, after an extensive period of travels both in India and abroad, Nanak settled at Kartarpur where he laid the foundation of the institution of the gurdwara which was originally called *dharmsala* (a place to practise righteousness). Nanak's *dharmsala* was quite distinct from that of traditional *dharmsalas* found throughout the Punjab at that time, which were houses where travellers could go to rest or spend the night. Nanak's *dharmsala*, however, became the focus for the transmission of his understanding of the notion of the oneness of God. At the *dharmsala* people would gather, irrespective of caste, creed and gender, and engage in communal worship and *shabad-kirtan* which was followed by a communal meal.

The term 'gurdwara' as such is attributed to the sixth guru, Hargobind, who is believed to have built gurdwaras on sites associated with his predecessors. Gurdwaras differ in size and shape but they all have the Guru Granth Sahib installed in them.

Another distinguishing feature of a gurdwara is the presence of the *nishan sahib* (Sikh flag) usually located near the building. Strictly speaking, a gurdwara is any building where a copy of the Guru Granth Sahib is installed.

There are mainly two types of gurdwaras: historic and community-based. Historic gurdwaras are those which have been erected on sites which are important landmarks in the history of the Sikh movement. For example, Gurdwara Sis Ganj in Delhi which is built on the spot where Guru Teg Bahadur was beheaded by the Mughul authorities, and Gurdwara Kesgarh at Anandpur where Guru Gobind Singh instituted the Khalsa.

COMMUNITY-BASED GURDWARAS

Over the centuries, community-based gurdwaras (often based in converted local houses) have been established to serve the local *sangats* in towns and villages as well as abroad. One of the distinguishing features of a community-based gurdwara is the nature of its management structure based on locally-elected management committees which are answerable to their *sangat* only, and are completely autonomous institutions.

Historic gurdwaras are controlled and managed by a central body called the Shiromani Gurdwara Parbandhak Committee (Supreme Management Committee of Gurdwaras). Its headquarters are located in the Golden Temple complex at Amritsar.

Family Gurdwaras

Many devout Sikh families keep a copy of the Guru Granth Sahib in their homes where a special room is reserved for the scriptures. Members of the family offer their reverence for the Guru Granth Sahib every day following certain ceremonial rules. Family gurdwaras, however, are not open to the general public. Although any building where a copy of the Guru Granth Sahib is installed qualifies to be called a gurdwara, a family gurdwara is strictly a private shrine.

Harimandir Sahib – 'The Golden Temple'

Harimandir Sahib is the central shrine of the Sikhs. The literal meaning of the word Harimandir is 'Temple of God'. It is also known as 'Darbar Sahib' (Divine Court) and the Golden Temple.

HISTORY OF THE GOLDEN TEMPLE

The Golden Temple – the Harimandir Sahib – was built by the fifth Guru, Arjun Dev, in the late sixteenth century, and finally completed in 1604. It stands in a rectangular reservoir called Amrit-Sarover (a reservoir containing water of immortality); it is approached by a causeway. Interestingly, the land on which the whole complex stands today was donated by the Mughul emperor, Akbar, to the third guru, Amar Das.

The temple has four doors symbolizing the omnipresence of God. It is open to all people, irrespective of caste, creed, colour and gender. Furthermore, it rejects the view that at the time of prayer, facing towards a particular direction has any special significance for understanding the divine gift of belonging to one human family. The architecture represents both the Islamic and Indic traditions: its perpendicular pillars symbolize traditional Indic style while the domes reflect the Muslim architectural tradition. In order to reinforce the notion of the oneness of God, Guru Arjun Dev invited Mian Mir, a devout Muslim saint, to lay the foundation stone of the new temple, and on its completion, Guru Arjun Dev installed in the Golden Temple the first copy of the Adi Granth.

A group of Sikhs inside a gurdwara in Vancouver standing behind the *palki* (palanquin) with the scriptures

Traditionally, most Sikh pilgrims bathe in the holy tank before entering the Golden Temple. A relay of religious musicians constantly sing hymns from the Guru Granth Sahib for twenty-one hours a day. It remains open throughout the day except for a short interval of three hours during the night from midnight to 4 am. During this period the floor is washed with a mixture of water and milk by the *sewadars* (volunteers) and is prepared to receive the Adi Granth which is brought in a procession from the Akal Takhat.

AKAL TAKHAT

The title Akal Takhat comprises two words: *Akal* meaning the Timeless God and *Takhat* denoting a throne, thus 'the throne of the Timeless God'. The Akal Takhat is a multi-storey structure. It was originally built by the sixth guru, Hargobind, in 1609 and faces the Golden Temple. Its establishment signifies the turning point in the history of the Sikh movement.

After the martyrdom of the fifth guru, Arjun Dev, in 1606, his son, Hargobind, took over the leadership. At his investiture, he wore two swords symbolising the doctrine of *miri* (temporal authority) and *piri* (spiritual authority). Under his leadership the Sikh movement accepted the challenge of the Mughul authorities and innovated a radical strategy of defending their faith. It is recorded how he sat on a raised platform in the Akal Takhat and issued *hukamnamas* ('orders of the day') to the Sikhs to bring horses and arms as *daswandh* (a tenth of one's earnings).

The Akal Takhat was reserved for discussing the

social and political concerns of the Sikh community while the Golden Temple represented the spiritual authority. During the eighteenth century, leaders of the Sikh *misls* (armies) used to meet at the Akal Takhat for formulating joint strategy against the Mughul forces.

These meetings were particularly known as the *Sarbat Khalsa*. They met in the presence of the Adi Granth and the resolutions approved at the meetings were called *gurmatas* ('guru's intention') which were binding on everyone present at the meetings. The Akal Takhat played a key role in the development of political consciousness among the Sikhs which, in 1799, resulted in the establishment of a sovereign Sikh state in the Punjab.

Five historic gurdwaras are designated as *takhats* (seat of authority) including the Akal Takhat which is the supreme *takhat* of the Sikh faith. The *hukamnamas* issued from the Akal Takhat are regarded as having the authority of the guru. During the period of British rule most socio-religious campaigns, such as the Gurdwara Reform Movement, were launched from the Akal Takhat.

In 1984, Sant Jarnail Singh Bhinderanwaley, the charismatic militant leader, launched his campaign for the establishment of Khalistan (independent Sikh state) from the Akal Takhat. The Indian army attacked the Akal Takhat to dislodge Bhinderanwaley and his followers; this action resulted in a considerable loss of life among both Sikhs and soldiers, and the virtual destruction of the Akal Takhat. The attack on the Akal Takhat generated profound feelings of resentment within the Sikh world. As a result, Indira Ghandi, the prime minister of India, was murdered by two of her Sikh bodyguards.

MANAGEMENT AND CONTROL

In 1920, the Sikhs formed the Shiromani Gurdwara Parbandhak Committee to gain control of the historic gurdwaras from the *mahants* (hereditary proprietors). In 1925, after a period of prolonged agitation, the British government passed the Punjab Sikh Gurdwaras Act and constituted the Shiromani Gurdwara Parbandhak Committee (SGPC). Since that time the SGPC has been responsible for the management of historic gurdwaras throughout the Punjab.

□

After the death of the tenth guru, Gobind Singh, the control of major historic gurdwaras passed into the hands of *mahants*. A considerable amount of land was attached to these gurdwaras which had been donated by Sikh royalty and Sikh devotees over the generations. Moreover, these gurdwaras were visited by a large number of Sikh pilgrims and were also a major source of income. The *mahants* not only misused the income but indulged in immoral activities within the precincts of the gurdwaras. Then, in an act which further infuriated the Sikhs, after the annexation of the Punjab, the British government granted the *mahants* the actual title of ownership

At the end of the First World War, the Sikhs launched a peaceful campaign popularly known as the Gurdwara Reform movement. In 1920 they appointed a committee under the name of the

Shiromani Gurdwara Parbandhak Committee to manage the historic gurdwaras. During this campaign a number of Sikh volunteers lost their lives and a significant number of Sikhs went to prison. Finally, in 1925 the British government agreed to the Sikh's demands and approved the Punjab Sikh Gurdwaras Act, and held elections to elect members of the officially constituted SGPC.

Definition of a Sikh

One of the significant aspects of the PSG Act was its definition of a Sikh person for preparing voting lists. It is in the form of a declaration which reads: 'I solemnly affirm that I am a Sikh, that I believe in the Guru Granth Sahib, that I believe in the Ten Gurus and that I have no other religion.'

The Punjab Sikh Gurdwaras Act of 1925 was hailed as a great victory by the Sikhs. The SGPC which might be described as a government within a government, is composed of 175 members who are elected every five years by the Sikh electorate. The SGPC emerged as a sort of Sikh parliament and its decisions acquired the sanctity of the *gurmata*. It is responsible for the administration of a number of educational institutions and hospitals in the Punjab. It also appoints the head of the Akal Takhat called *Jathedar* who is a paid official of the SGPC.

NISHAN SAHIB – THE SIKH FLAG

One of the distinguishing features of a gurdwara is the *nishan sahib* flying above it. It is a triangular flag with the Khalsa emblem of Khanda: it is the insignia of the Khalsa comprising a double-edged sword fixed in a steel circle with two curved swords. The flag and the covering (*chola*) are made of saffron-coloured material.

The ceremony of *nishan sahib chardna* (replacing the old covering) takes place on the festival of Baisakhi which usually falls on 13 April each year. The ceremony begins with the recital of *ardas* (Sikh prayer). First, the mast is carefully lowered and the covering is removed. Next, the mast is ritually washed with a mixture of milk and water and dried with clean towels, and then the new covering is put on it. As soon as the mast with the new flag is in place, a member of the Sikh *sangat* chants the Sikh slogan: *Boley so nihal-sat sri akal* ('Anyone who utters the name of God is immortal and is a happy person.')

New coverings for the *nishan sahib* come as donations from the Sikh community (families). The ritual washing of the mast symbolizes its religious status; in effect, it is treated as a holy person. The term *chola* (covering) denotes a long loose saffron shirt worn by holy men which further signifies the sanctity attributed to the flag. Before entering the gurdwara, Sikhs bow towards the *nishan sahib* and touch the base of the mast as a symbol of respect and reverence.

KIRTAN – RELIGIOUS SINGING

Kirtan (religious singing) is an integral part of a Sikh service which always begins with *shabad-kirtan* (singing hymns from the scriptures). It is performed by the *ragis* (religious musicians) playing drums and a harmonium. The tradition of *shabad-kirtan* was innovated by Guru Nanak. Nanak composed his *bani* (writings) in a poetic form while his companion Mardana, a Muslim minstrel (p.18), provided the musical setting and then both sang together throughout their travels.

At the end of his missionary travels, Nanak settled at Kartarpur where his followers would gather at his house for congregational worship that began with the *shabad-kirtan*. Nanak was not only a poet but an accomplished musician.

It is important to note that a Sikh service begins with the recital and singing of *Asa di Var* in all gurdwaras following the procedure established by Guru Nanak. The significance of the *kirtan* is clearly manifested at the Golden Temple where worship begins with the recital and singing of *Asa di Var*, followed by the singing of hymns from the Adi Granth which continues throughout the day. The tradition of *shabad-kirtan* was meticulously observed and developed by Nanak's successors. Moreover, the compiler of the Adi Granth, Guru Arjun Dev, prescribed and recorded the musical setting to which the hymns should be sung.

□

All Sikh gurus used the services of Muslim musicians called *rababis* during their ministry. Bhai Balwand and Bhai Satta were the first *rababis* to perform *shabad-kirtan* at the Golden Temple under the patronage of Guru Arjun Dev. The sixth guru, Hargobind, employed two Muslim *dhadis* (musician who plays the instrument of *dhad*, a double-headed drum) who sang martial ballads at the Akal Takhat. The *rababis* continued performing *shabad-kirtan* at the Golden Temple until the partition of India in 1947.

Nowadays, the Shiromani Gurdwara Parbandhak Committee (SGPC) employ professional Sikh *ragis* (musicians who are also known as *kirtanias*) to perform *shabad-kirtan* at the historic gurdwaras in the Punjab. Most community-based gurdwaras employ full-time *granthis* (reader of the Adi Granth) who usually perform *shabad-kirtan* as well. Although all *ragis* employed by the gurdwaras are Sikh, the descendants of Mardana are invited by the Sikhs to perform in India as well as abroad. The *shabad-kirtan* plays a fundamental role in transmitting the message of the *gurbani* (scriptures) to the *sangat*.

□

The tradition of *rein sabai kirtan* is similar to the traditional *jagrata* (singing of hymns dedicated to the Mother Goddess) in Hinduism. A *rein sabai kirtan* is organized by the gurdwaras once or twice a year. It usually begins at 7.00pm and culminates in the early hours of the morning. A relay of *ragis* take part in the *rein sabai kirtan*. The *langar* is prepared for the *sangat* which is served all night.

SAT SANG IN SIKH HOMES

Most devout Sikh families organize *sat sang* (literally, the company of holy persons) at their homes. They invite local *ragis* to perform the *shabad-kirtan*. They prepare *langar* for the *sangat*. A *sat sang* usually lasts two to three hours, and

A group of Sikh ladies taking part in *shabad-kirtan* (religious singing)

A Sikh holy person leading the *shabad-kirtan* during congregational worship

culminates with a Sikh prayer and a communal meal. Another interesting development is the popularity of the 'Ladies *Sat Sang*'. Strictly speaking, everyone can participate in a Ladies *Sat Sang* but it is primarily a women's gathering. The *shabad-kirtan* is performed by Sikh women most of whom are amateur singers. Sikh women also participate in the *shabad-kirtan* at gurdwaras.

Ardas – Sikh prayer

Ardas is an essential part of Sikh worship. All acts of worship and ceremonies such as weddings, initiation or *arkhand-path* (unbroken reading of the Adi Granth) begin and culminate with *ardas*. The term *ardas* is the Punjabi version of the Persian word *arz-dasht*; it is composed of two words: *arz* (request or supplication) and *dasht* (to present or to submit). Thus, it means presenting one's plea or request.

At the time of *ardas* the whole congregation stands with folded hands and concentrates on the recital of *ardas*. Generally, the *granthi* of a gurdwara recites *ardas* but it can be recited by any Sikh.

The present *ardas* is a standardized version approved by the Shiromani Gurdwara Parbandhak Committee. Before the recital of *ardas* the whole congregation sings the verse '*tum thakur tum pah ardas*' (You are the Lord whom I pray. . .) (AD 268). Then *ardas* begins by invoking God and uttering 'There is One God and Glory to God'. It is believed that the original *ardas* was composed by Guru Gobind Singh whose name is chanted at the start of the recital of *ardas*. The first part of *ardas* concentrates on remembering God, the Ten Gurus, the Guru Granth Sahib, and the glorious deeds of the *pani pyarey* (first five Sikhs initiated by Guru Gobind Singh), and the tenth guru's four sons and other martyrs. Finally, a special plea is offered for the well-being of the whole of humankind.

At the culmination of the main *ardas* a short couplet is sung by the whole congregation; it reinforces the belief that all Sikhs are mandated to revere the Adi Granth as their guru, ending with the Sikh slogan: '*Wahe Guru ji ka Khalsa, Wahe Guru ji ki Fateh*' (The Khalsa belongs to God, and victory to God.) The congregation then sits down and awaits for the *hukamnama*. The *granthi* opens the Adi Granth at random and recites the first hymn on the left-hand page; it is regarded as Guru's order for the day. The service ends with the distribution of *karah-parshad* (sanctified food) to the members of the congregation.

KARAH-PARSHAD – SANCTIFIED FOOD

The term *karah-parshad* is composed of two words: *karah* means an iron pan and *parshad* denotes food offered to a deity; hence sanctified food cooked in an iron pan. The word *parshad* also means 'grace' signifying the sacredness of the food. Another respectable name for *karah-parshad* is *deg* (literally a cooking pot, food for offering). *Karah-parshad* is always received in cupped hands as a gift of God. No Sikh will leave a gurdwara without receiving a portion of *karah-parshad* for those members of the family who are not able to visit the gurdwara either because of illness or because they are engaged in domestic duties.

Karah-parshad is made of equal parts of whole-meal flour, sugar and *ghee* (clarified butter). Many Sikhs make offerings of wheatflour, sugar and butter to the gurdwara for the *karah-parshad* whereas some families would donate cash particularly for the *deg* (*karah-parshad*).

The preparation of the *karah-parshad* is regarded as a sacred ritual. II is always prepared in a clean kitchen. Usually, it is cooked by a *granthi* who takes a bath before starting the preparations. During the whole operation he recites *gurbani* (compositions from the Adi Granth). Nobody is allowed to interfere during the preparation of *karah-parshad*.

Once the food is ready it is carried by a Sikh over his head to the congregational hall and placed next to the scriptures. During the recital of *ardas*, a special plea is made for God's blessing of *karah-parshad*. At that moment an attendant Sikh stirs the *karah-parshad* with a small sword which signifies fulfilment of the plea. Before the food is distributed to members of the congregation, it is ritually offered to five *amritdhari* (initiated) Sikhs symbolizing the authority of the Guru.

6 Festivals

Festival of Diwali

GURPURB

Sikh festivals fall into two main categories: *gurpurb* and *mela*. The term *gurpurb* is composed of two words: *gur* short of 'guru' and *purb* which denotes a sacred or auspicious day. The term *gurpurb* is applied to anniversaries when gurus are remembered. There are four main *gurpurbs* celebrated by Sikhs through-out the world. These are the birthday anniversaries of gurus Nanak and Gobind Singh, and the martyrdom-day anniversaries of gurus Arjun Dev and Teg Bahadur. The Guru Granth Sahib is at the centre of Sikh festivals. A *gurpurb* celebration begins with the *akhand-path* (unbroken reading of the Adi Granth) and concludes with *diwan* (congregational worship). *Langar* is served twenty-four hours a day during the *akhand-path* ceremony.

In India *gurpurbs* are celebrated by taking Guru Granth Sahib in processions called *jaloos* in villages and towns. In villages, the Guru Granth Sahib is placed in a decorated *palki* (palanquin) which is carried by Sikh *sewadars* (volunteers). A procession is led by five Sikhs carrying swords symbolizing *panj-pyarey* (five Sikhs originally initiated by Gobind Singh in 1699). Members of the *sangat* march behind the *palki* singing hymns.

Many gurdwaras in Britain organize processions to mark the festival of *Baisakhi*. Martyrdom day of Arjun Dev falls in the months of May-June. Local Sikh *sangats* set up *shabeels* (stalls) offering cold soft drinks such as *sharbat*, a mixture of milk, sugar and water, orange juice and Coca Cola which is served to the general public. People are politely requested by the volunteers to share cold drinks as a mark of remembrance.

MELA

The word *mela* literally means a fair. Sikh *melas* are both religious and cultural celebrations. Sikhs share a common cultural heritage with the Hindus and celebrate a number of important Indic festivals such as Diwali, Baisakhi and Holi with a marked difference in content and style. As tradition relates, Guru Amar Das began to encourage Sikhs to gather at his village on major Hindu festivals instead of making offerings to the Hindu Brahmins. In fact, it was the beginning of a new and distinct community in the Punjab.

DIWALI

Diwali is popularly known as the Festival of Light. Hindus illuminate their homes and temples ritually celebrating the home-coming of Lord Rama from exile. Traditionally, earthen *divas* (small oil lamps) were used by people. Gifts of Indian sweets are exchanged by friends and families. Mounds of Indian sweets are sold and bought on the festival of *diwali*. It is also a New Year day in the Indian calendar. Hindu craftsmen worship their tools on the following day; it is called Vishvakarma *puja* (worship of Lord Vishvakarma, deity of Hindu craftsmen).

The festival of *diwali* has another significance for Sikhs. It is associated with the release of Guru Hargobind from the Gowalior Fort where he was imprisoned by the Mughul Emperor Jehangir. The guru's arrival in Amritsar was celebrated by illuminating the Golden Temple and their own houses. Nowadays, gurdwaras and houses are decorated with candles and rows of lights, and firework displays are organized as part of the celebrations, as in Amritsar. In Britain and elsewhere the diaspora Sikhs take Indian sweets to their gurdwara as part of their offerings where the celebrations culminate with an evening *diwan* and display of fireworks.

BAISAKHI

The festival of *Baisakhi* is celebrated on the first day of the month of *Baisakh* in the Punjabi calendar;

hence, it is New Year's day in the Punjab. Traditionally, farmers begin harvesting the wheat crop after the *Baisakhi* celebrations. *Baisakhi* has a special significance for Sikhs. In 1699 the tenth guru, Gobind Singh, founded the institution of the Khalsa brotherhood on the *Baisakhi* day which is associated with re-generation and new life. The ritual of replacing the covering of the *nishan-sahib* is performed as part of *Baisakhi*.

The cultural dimension of the festival of *Baisakhi* is celebrated by organizing team games such as football, hockey and *kabadi*. Display of individual skill and strength is demonstrated by wrestlers and experts in the martial arts. Traditional Bhangra dancing is the climax of the *Baisakhi* celebrations when dancers dress up in colourful Punjabi costumes. They are accompanied by Punjabi folk music and a *dhole* (a large double-edged drum).

HOLA

The festival of *Hola* takes its name from the Hindu festival of *Holi* which is celebrated by throwing colours on people irrespective of gender and status. Guru Gobind Singh disapproved of the nature of the *Holi* festival and regarded it as a wasteful exercise. Instead, he introduced the tradition of *Hola*.

Gobind Singh summoned the Sikhs to Anandpur to celebrate the festival of *Holi* in a different way. He organized mock battles between two groups of Sikh volunteers and trained them in the martial arts, thereby giving them a new purpose in life. The title of the festival was changed to *Hola*.

Southall, London: 300th anniversary celebrations (1999) of the Baisakhi festival marking the founding of the Khalsa

Hola is one of the most colourful festivals held at Anandpur every year. Sikh bands display their skills in the traditional martial arts as part of the huge procession that marks the culmination of the festival. Sikhs come from all over India to join in the celebrations which last for several days. Political parties of the Punjab organize their public conferences during the *Hola* celebrations at Anandpur.

SANGRAND

The first day of every month in the Hindu lunar calendar is called *Sangrand*. *Sangrand* is the Punjabi version of the Sanskrit term *sangkrant* which denotes the entrance of the sun into a new sign of the Zodiac. On this day Hindu Brahmins visit the home of their clients in villages to announce the beginning of the new month and receive customary payment in kind such as wheat and raw sugar.

Sangrand is regarded as an auspicious day. It is observed by holding special *diwan* at gurdwaras for ritually announcing the name of the new month from the Adi Granth. Guru Arjun Dev composed the hymn of *Bara Maha* (literally the hymn of twelve months). It comprises twelve hymns collectively called the *Bara Maha*. Each hymn illustrates the stages of life and the journey of the soul while directing the Sikhs to conform to a specific code of discipline during each month. Sikhs visit gurdwaras on this festival day before setting off to work. Interestingly, the festival of *Baisakhi* occurs at *Sangrand* in the month of *Baisakh*.

7 The *Khalsa*

Amrit – the ceremony of Sikh initiation

The term *Khalsa* is applied to the community of initiated (*amritdhari*) Sikhs established by the tenth guru, Gobind Singh, at Anandpur in 1699. The nucleus of this new dynamic community is popularly known as *panj pyarey* (five beloved ones) who volunteered to sacrifice their lives for the sake of the guru on the fateful day of *Baisakhi*. Thereafter, the title 'Khalsa' is reserved for initiated Sikhs only. In fact, the founding of the *Khalsa* is the beginning of a distinctive Sikh identity which had enormous impact on the future development of the Sikh tradition overall.

The word *Khalsa* is derived from the Arabic *khalis* meaning pure or unadulterated; it also refers to the

Picture of the *Panj-pyarey* (Five Beloved Ones) in traditional uniform leading a procession in the UK

land that was under the direct control c
Both these meanings provide deep in:
strategic planning of Guru Gobind Singl
ing the institution of the *Khalsa*. He wa
eliminating internal divisions within the S:
by creating a central authority under his direct
control. At the same time, he was confronted with
the repressive policies of the Mughul administration
which was determined to destroy the Sikh movement
for good.

HISTORICAL CONTEXT

Tradition focuses on two main factors which were
crucial to the founding of the *Khalsa*. The first is
directly related to the death and manner of execution
of the ninth guru, Teg Bahadur, who in 1675 was
publicly beheaded at Delhi on the orders of Emperor
Aurangzeb. The second reason was the cowardly
behaviour of those Sikhs who were present at the
time of the execution and did not come forward to
remove the guru's body and severed head. Instead,
they drew back to avoid recognition for fear of
persecution by the authorities. At that time one could
not distinguish a Sikh just from his appearance.

Another major threat came from the *masands* (the
guru's nominated officials) who had become the main
cause of the internal strife within the Sikh movement.
Many *masands* had established themselves as gurus
and refused to acknowledge the authority of the tenth
guru, Gobind Singh.

ᴊAKHI DAY

According to tradition, Gobind Singh issued special invitations to the Sikhs with a directive to gather at Anandpur on the occasion of the festival of *Baisakhi*. A large number of Sikhs from all over India responded to his call. It is believed that Gobind Singh appeared before the huge gathering just after the culmination of the morning service. He had his sword in his hand and demanded the head of a Sikh for sacrifice. After some hesitation, one Sikh came forward – he was taken into a tent by the guru. A little later, the guru reappeared with his sword dripping with blood and demanded another volunteer. In this way five men were taken into the tent to be sacrificed.

Then, to everybody's amazement, the guru came out of the tent with the five volunteers who were wearing saffron-coloured clothes like those of the guru. Then the guru declared that the *panj pyarey* (Five Beloved Ones) were to be the nucleus of a new and dynamic community called the *Khalsa*. This description of the founding of the *Khalsa* forms the main focus of the *Baisakhi* celebrations in the gurdwaras.

AMRIT – SIKH INITIATION

Amrit literally means water of immortality which is used in the Sikh initiation ceremony; it is known as *khande di pahul* (literally, water of the double-edged sword). Let us go back to the fateful day of *Baisakhi* in 1699. After the selection of *panj pyarey*, the guru prepared *amrit* for the initiation ceremony. He discarded the centuries-old tradition of *charan pahul*. Before the founding of the *Khalsa*, the initiation used to be conducted with water touched by a guru's toe, thus the term *charan pahul* (*charan* means foot, *pahul* denotes water).

The new-style initiation ceremony was fundamentally different from the traditional mode of initiation. Preparation of *amrit* is one of the defining factors of the new rite.. The guru poured water into a steel bowl and stirred it with a double-edged sword while reciting hymns from the Adi Granth, including some of his own compositions. It is said that the guru's wife added some sugar into the bowl during the preparation of *amrit*.

The five volunteers who belonged to different caste groups drank *amrit* from the same bowl signifying their entry into the casteless fraternity of the *Khalsa*. At the initiation ceremony, *panj pyarey* took the following vows:

1. My father is Guru Gobind Singh.
2. My mother is Mata Sahib Devan (wife of Guru Gobind Singh).
3. My place of birth is Anandpur.

These vows further reinforced the notion of the corporate *Khalsa* brotherhood.

'SINGH' AND 'KAUR'

After the *amrit* ceremony, the next most significant innovation was the change in their names. All five volunteers, like the guru, had traditional Hindu names before their initiation. Now they were given a new corporate name 'Singh'.

The Meaning of 'Singh'

The word Singh is derived from the Sanskrit *simbha* meaning lion; it had been in common use as a surname by Hindu princes in India. Thus the guru elevated the status of ordinary people to that of the Kshatriyas (warrior and princely caste group).

It was the climax of the *amrit* ceremony when the guru received *amrit* from the *panj pyarey* and changed his name from Gobind Rai to Gobind Singh. It is important to note that Guru Gobind Singh admitted women into the *Khalsa*. After the initiation, a woman receives the name 'Kaur' which means a princess.

Names of the *panij pyarey*

Before Initiation	After Initiation
1. Daya Ram	1. Daya Singh
2. Dharam Das	2. Dharam Singh
3. Mohkam Chand	3. Mohkam Singh
4. Sahib Chand	4. Sahib Singh
5. Himat Rai	5. Himat Singh

□

THE *AMRIT* CEREMONY:

1. It initiated the birth of a distinctive corporate identity within the Sikh movement.
2. It removed the fear of death from the minds of the new initiates.
3. By admitting women into the *Khalsa* brotherhood it reinforced the Sikh belief in the equality of humankind.

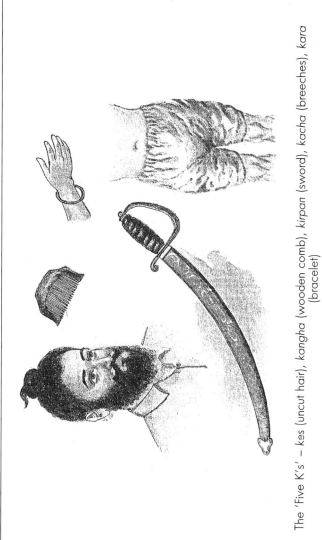

The 'Five K's' – kes (uncut hair), kangha (wooden comb), kirpan (sword), kacha (breeches), kara (bracelet)

4. It innovated a new style *amrit/khande di pahul* ceremony which can be conducted only by five *amritdhari* Sikhs symbolizing the institution of *panj pyarey* (five beloved ones).
5. It deprived the *masands* of the privilege of conducting initiation ceremonies and established the authority of the institution of the *panj pyarey* as representatives of the guru.

Khalsa – code of discipline

According to tradition, Guru Gobind Singh prescribed a new code of discipline for the members of the *Khalsa*. It includes the wearing of five emblems collectively known as *panj kakke* (Five K's). They are:

1. **kes** (uncut hair)
2. **kangha** (a small wooden comb worn in the hair)
3. **kirpan** (a sword, nowadays a small sword is worn by Sikhs)
4. **kacha/kachhahira** (a pair of knee-length breeches)
5. **kara** (a steel bracelet/circle worn on the right wrist)

Since the names of Sikh emblems begin with the letter 'kakka' of the *Gurumukhi* script they are known as the five 'kakke'. The letter *kakka* corresponds to K of the Roman alphabet, thus, 'the five K's'.

Afterwards, the guru described four rules of conduct for members of the *Khalsa*: he/she must not cut hair and must not smoke or chew tobacco and consume alcohol. They should not eat *halal* meat, slaughtered according to Muslim customs, but only *jhatka* meat, where the animal has been slaughtered with one blow. Finally, they must not molest a Muslim woman.

A detailed and comprehensive code of discipline was approved by the Shiromani Gurdwara Parbandhak Committee in 1945; it is called the *Rahit Maryada* (a guide to the Sikh way of life).

Although a turban is not one of the prescribed emblems, it has far greater significance for Sikhs than any other head-covering as it is used to cover the hair (*kes*). A male Sikh is required to wear the turban in public which is regarded as a symbol of honour.

□

A Sikh who has been initiated into the *Khalsa* is called *amritdhari*. The distinction between *amritdhari* Sikhs and non-*amritdhari* Sikhs occurred after the founding of the *Khalsa* in 1699. Non-*amritdhari* Sikhs, like the gurus, had Hindu names, and there was no particular prescribed rules for admittance into the Sikh fold. The main requirement of becoming a Sikh was one's loyalty to the gurus and belief in their teachings, such as participation in congregational worship, sharing a communal meal, engaging in acts of service to the community and making offerings to the guru in the form of *daswandh* (one tenth of one's earnings reserved for the guru's *golak* (cash chest).

The status of *amritdhari* Sikh is regarded as an ideal within the Sikh community. Sikhs are expected to take *amrit* sometime in their life. At the wedding ceremony the couple are advised to become *amritdharis* whenever it is convenient. The overwhelming majority of Sikhs are non-*amritdharis*.

KESDHARI SIKHS

A Sikh person who keeps his/her hair unshorn and observes a standard code of discipline, except the initiation ceremony, is called *kesdhari*. The word *kes* means hair whilst the term *dhari* denotes 'wearer'. It is important to note that all *amritdhari* Sikhs are *kesdharis* whereas *kesdhari* may not be an *amritdhari*. The distinguishing feature between the two identities is the *amrit* (initiation) which requires the wearing of five emblems (5 K's) by the *Khalsa*.

□

Let us now consider two important definitions of a Sikh which provide insight into the process by which the *Rahit* (Sikh code of discipline) evolved. We have already discussed the situation during the pre-*Khalsa* period when there were no formal requirements for entry into the Sikh Panth. Strictly speaking, there was no agreed Sikh code of discipline until the passing of the *Rahit Maryada* (a guide to the Sikh way of life) by the Shiromani Gurdwara Parbandhak Committee in 1945. It defines a Sikh as under:

'A Sikh is any person whose faith is in one God, the ten Gurus and their teachings and the Adi Granth. In addition, he or she must believe in the necessity and importance of *amrit* (initiation) and must not adhere to any other religion.' Most importantly, this definition does not make any distinction between a *kesdhari*, an *amritdhari* or a *sahajdhari* Sikh.

The significant part of this injunction is the requirement of belief in the necessity of *amrit*. Although the definition of a Sikh in the *Rahit Maryada* applies to the great majority of Sikhs, it does not include those who believe in the tradition of a living guru like the Namdhari Sikhs.

Finally, let us look at the definition of a Sikh person as recorded in the Delhi Gurdwara Act of 1971. It reads:

'"Sikh" means a person who professes the Sikh religion, believes and follows the teachings of Sri Guru Granth Sahib and the ten Gurus only, and keeps unshorn hair. For the purposes of this Act, if any question arises as to whether any living person is or is not a Sikh, he shall be deemed respectively to be or not to be a Sikh according as he makes or refuses to make in the manner prescribed by rules the following declaration:-
"I solemnly affirm and declare that I am a *Keshadhari* Sikh, that I believe in and follow the teachings of Sri Guru Granth Sahib and, the ten Gurus only, and that I have no other religion".'

A close examination of the three definitions of a Sikh person indicates the developmental process concerning *Rahit Maryada* of the Sikh community. For example, the definition provided in the Punjab Sikh Gurdwaras Act of 1925 is much more liberal and inclusive than the other two. It reflects the religious and political environment of the 1920s when the Sikh movement was engaged in a bitter struggle against the British government and the *masands* for the control of the historic gurdwaras.

SAHAJDHARI SIKHS

The term 'Sahajdhari' is applied to non-Khalsa Sikhs. Strictly speaking, it includes Kesdhari and clean-shaven (mona) Sikhs. The word sahaj means 'slow' or 'natural' and the term Sahajdhari denotes 'slow adopter' or a Sikh who is on the way to becoming a Khalsa Sikh. The problem of defining Sikh identity is a complex one. Originally, people chose to enter the Sikh Panth but nowadays children born into Sikh families are regarded as Sikhs. Many Sikhs cut their hair and trim their beards but their commitment to the Sikh tradition is equally strong.

According to McLeod: 'The term Sahajdhari was applied during the eighteenth century to Sikhs who cut their hair, and is used in precisely this sense by the Chaupa Singh Rahitnama.' A number of Sahajdhari Sikhs played important roles within the Sikh movement in the eighteenth century. For example, Bhai (highly respectable title applied to prominent Sikhs) Des Raj was put in charge of rebuilding the Golden Temple in 1764 after its destruction by the Muslim invader, Ahmad Shah, in 1762. Bhai Des Raj was also granted a seal (Guru di Mohar, literally guru's seal) to collect more funds for the project.

Many Sindhi (belonging to the province of Sindh now in Pakistan) Sikh families are Sahajdhari, and most of them have Hindu names. The category of amritdhari Sikhs emerged at the Baisakhi festival of 1699. All Sikhs before that day were simply known as Sikhs of the guru to whom we now apply the term Sahajdhari.

8 Rites of Passage

A Sikh wedding ceremony

BIRTH

The birth of a child is regarded as *waheguru di dat* (gift of God). After marriage the birth of a child is eagerly awaited by the parents of the young couple. Punjabi Sikh society is patriarchal and all inheritance is through the male line. The birth of a son ensures that he will perform the funeral rites to save his parents' soul. On the birth of a son there is great rejoicing and an exchange of gifts, whereas the arrival of a daughter remains a comparatively quiet affair.

Usually, the first child is born at the wife's parental home (*nanke*). For a son, the doors of a house are decorated with leaves from the *sirin* (Acacia Sirissa) or mango tree. The festival of *Lohrdi* and the ceremony of *chhati* are celebrated on the birth of a son. The festival of *Lohrdi* falls in the month of January. The family distributes Indian sweets (*reordi*) and roasted groundnuts among relatives and members of the *biradari* (caste). In the evening a huge bonfire is organized by the family. Women of the household and the *biradari* get together to sing songs celebrating the birth of a boy.

The ceremony of *chhati* usually takes place five weeks after the birth of a son. This involves a big feast organized by the paternal family to which the mother's parents, other relatives and members of one's *biradari* are invited. The mother and child receive gifts from their parents, relatives and members of the *biradari*. The celebration of *Lohrdi* and *chhati* reinforces traditional values among the Sikhs.

Boys and girls are prepared for their distinct roles within the family. A girl learns to cook and sew as well as look after any younger brothers and sisters; a boy, on the other hand, is trained to take over his father's role by pursuing outdoor activities. However, there has been a major shift in the attitude of Sikh parents both in India and throughout the diaspora. For example, in Britain boys and girls receive free and compulsory education up to the end of secondary school, while the number of Sikh girls attending institutions of Further and Higher Education has been growing rapidly, though boys are still given preferential treatment by their parents.

NAMING

Traditionally, children are given names by their grandparents or by their *bhua* (father's sister). Nowadays, most Sikh families go to the gurdwara and ask for an initial letter of the *Gurmukhi* alphabet from the Adi Granth in order to choose the name. The first letter of the *hukamnama* (order of the day) hymn is used to choose the name. Usually, the name is announced at the gurdwara on the following Sunday. Devout Sikh families ensure that a new-born baby receives *amrit* (ritually prepared nectar). The *granthi* (reader of the Adi Granth) recites the first five verses of the Adi Granth while stirring the water and sugar with a *Khanda* (double-edged sword). He then puts some *amrit* into the baby's mouth with a *kirpan* (miniature ceremonial sword).

'Singh' and 'Kaur'

The name-titles 'Singh' and 'Kaur' were first prescribed by the tenth guru, Gobind Singh, in 1699. Nowadays, children born into Sikh families automatically get the name-title 'Singh' and 'Kaur' after their first name. All male Sikhs have 'Singh' while all female Sikhs have 'Kaur' with their first name, e.g. Mohinder Singh and Jaswinder Kaur.

TURBAN

Although a turban is not one of the five emblems of the *Khalsa*, it is an essential part of a male Sikh's uniform. It is also worn by many Muslim and Hindu men in the sub-continent; it is both a garment and a symbol of honour. Men in many Middle Eastern countries also wear turbans.

There is no specific injunction concerning the age at which one starts wearing a turban. Usually, a Sikh boy begins to wear a turban when he reaches the age of eleven or twelve and is able to look after it. Turbans may be of any colour. The elderly, as well as East African Sikhs, prefer to wear white turbans. Members of the Akali Party (political party of the Sikhs) wear blue turbans while the saffron colour is associated with the *Khalsa*. Normally, a turban is made of muslin cloth and is five yards in length.

Nowadays, many Sikh families organize *pagri bananan* (tying a turban) ceremony for their young sons. It is normally performed at a gurdwara or at the family's residence in the presence of the Adi Granth. After the *ardas* (Sikh prayer), the *granthi*, or another prominent Sikh, is asked to tie the turban on the boy's head. The congregation chant *boley so nihal – sat sri akal* (one who says God is immortal is a happy person) signifying approval and joy. Families make generous donations of cash and food to the gurdwara and the young man receives gifts from his parents and relatives.

A turban signifies the religious identity of a male Sikh. An insult to the turban is regarded as an insult to the Sikh faith because the turban covers and controls the *kes*, one of the five emblems of the *Khalsa* code of discipline. In Britain, the USA and Canada Sikhs had to fight for the right to wear turbans at work. In the UK, turbaned Sikhs have been exempted from wearing crash helmets.

HOW TO TIE A TURBAN

Usually an adult turban is five yards long and 36-45 inches wide. The length is smoothly turned around the head six times by clockwise movements of the hands. Both ends of the 'length' or turban must be tucked in properly - i.e. the beginning or finishing ends of the turban should not be flowing loosely as can be seen with many non-Sikh Indian turbans.

STEP ONE - Fold the turban cloth of a suitable length to about three and a half inches thick.

STEP FOUR - Repeat this pattern until the cloth has gone around your head five times. *(Figure 3 & 4)*

3 & 4

STEP TWO - Hold one end of the cloth near your left shoulder, take the rest of the cloth around the back of your head near the joora and bring it down towards the right ear. *(Figure 1)*

1

STEP FIVE - Take the remaining cloth around your head for the last time and tuck it at the front of the turban so that it cannot be seen. *(Figure 5)*

5

STEP THREE - Take the cloth around your head again but slightly away from the Joora and bring it back down to the left ear just above the first layer of cloth. *(Figure 2)*

2

STEP SIX - From the top of the head pull out the bottom layer of cloth next to the joora and open it out. Once the cloth is opened, cover the joora and any other visible hair. *(Figure 6)*

6

STEP SEVEN - Take the loose end you first began with and tuck it into the back of the turban. *(Figure 7)*

7

And there, you have a beautiful Turban

(figure 8).

by Rupinder Kaur Chana
Ramgarhia Sunday School

MARRIAGE

The institution of marriage is regarded as the bedrock of Sikh society. Guru Nanak taught his followers that they should lead a worldly life, that is, the normal life of householders, recognizing their duties to parents, wife and children and to the wider society. He rejected the notion of asceticism and celibacy. A Sikh wedding has far greater significance than the simple unification of man and woman; it is regarded as an alliance between two families of compatible social and caste status.

The scriptures consider marriage to be a spiritual bond, and emphasize the concept of *ek jote doye murti* (one soul in two bodies). Moreover, the concept of *sanjog* (relationship preordained by God) plays an important role in the establishment of a marriage alliance.

ARRANGED MARRIAGES

Traditionally, in Punjabi Sikh society, marriages are arranged by the parents. The most important area in which parents have control over their children is the selection of spouses. Marriages are arranged according to the rules of caste endogamy according to which 'correct' partners can be found only in one's own caste group.

Since the institution of marriage plays an important role in maintaining boundaries between caste groups, inter-caste marriages are strongly disapproved of; the partners in such alliances are treated as outsiders and a stain on the family honour.

The process of arranging a marriage begins when the parents ask their relatives to look for a suitable spouse for their son or daughter. It was customary to arrange marriages of fairly young children. Nowadays, the marriages are arranged as soon as children complete their education. A person who arranges the *rishta* (marital alliance) is called a *bichola* (match-maker). He provides vital information about the would-be bride and groom including the general reputation and caste status of the families concerned.

Marriage negotiations are conducted in complete secrecy to avoid any embarrassment to the two families. Once the formal matching of caste status and the suitability of spouses are agreed upon, the girl's parents ask the matchmaker to arrange a meeting with the boy's family in order to 'see' (*munda dekhna*) the boy. Nowadays, the respective families meet both the girl and boy. Most Sikh parents insist on arranging a preliminary meeting between the spouses in order to seek their approval before finalizing the marital bond.

Once the families have approved the relationship, a date is fixed for the engagement ceremony of *mangni/kurmai*. It takes place at the boy's residence or at a local gurdwara. A party of five or seven kinsmen of the girl, usually her father, father's brothers and maternal uncles, go to perform the engagement ceremony. They take gifts of *mathyai* (Indian sweets) and fresh fruit with them. The ceremony takes place in the presence of male relatives and members of one's *biradari* (caste). It begins with the recital of *ardas* If the ceremony is conducted at the gurdwara, a special hymn of *kurmai* is recited from the Adi Granth, and a *hukamnama* is read out.

Now the girls' father puts seven handfuls of dried fruit in the boys *jholi* (lap made of a pink scarf) and then he puts one *chhuara* (dried date) in the boy's mouth. This ritual is called *sagan dena* (giving a ritual gift), and it confirms the acceptance of the relationship by both families and their relatives and members of their *biradari*. The boy receives gifts of a golden bracelet and some cash from the girl's father. Other relatives also make gifts of cash to the boy.

Following the engagement ceremony, the boy's family sends gifts of a long scarf (*chuni*) and sweets for the would-be bride. The sweets are distributed among close relatives and members of the *biradari* as an announcement of the engagement of their daughter.

WEDDING CEREMONY

The date of the wedding ceremony is fixed by mutual agreement. It is customary to send a *sahey chithi* (invitation letter) to the boy's family, formally inviting them to the solemnization of the marriage on an appointed day. The *sahey chithi* is prepared in the presence of close relatives and members of the *biradari*, and it is sprinkled with saffron. This custom has a ritual significance since red is the symbol of the renewal of life. In the Punjab, it used to be the customary duty of the family *nai* (barber) to deliver *sahey chithi*, for which he received a ritual gift of clothes and some cash. In the diaspora, the *sahey chithi* is delivered by the *bichola* (matchmaker).

PRE-WEDDING RITUALS

1. *MAYIAN*

Two days before the wedding, the ritual of *mayian* is performed at the couple's respective homes. The prospective bride or groom is seated on a wooden plank called a *patri*, and a red cloth is held above by four female relatives, while married women of the household and *biradari*, led by the mother, rub paste of turmeric, flour and mustard oil on his/her face, arms and legs. During this ritual women sing traditional songs and those of the *biradari* receive the ritual gift of *gogley* (Punjabi sweets specially cooked for weddings) at the end of the ceremony.

2. *CHURA*

On the day before the wedding, a ritual of *chura* (involving a set of ivory bangles) is performed at the would-be bride's residence. Her maternal uncle makes a gift of clothes, jewellery and some cash called *nankey-shak*. He puts the bangles on his niece while the women sing traditional songs depicting the role of maternal uncle. Before the wedding ceremony, the bride-to-be takes a ritual bath and wears clothes provided by her maternal uncle, and she gets wed in those clothes. Similarly, the bridegroom-to-be also receives a set of clothes called *jora-jama* from his maternal uncle which he, too, wears at the wedding ceremony. It signifies the importance of the role of the mother's natal family at the wedding rituals, which also reinforces the alliance established at her (mother's) own wedding.

BARAT (WEDDING PARTY)

Traditionally, the wedding party consisted of the groom accompanied by male relatives and members of the *biradari*. Nowadays, women also attend. The wedding party is received by the kinsmen of the bride at a *janjgarh* (hall reserved for wedding parties) or a gurdwara where the ceremony of *milni* (ritual meeting of the heads of both families) takes place in the presence of relatives and members of one's *biradari*.

MILNI

The ceremony of *milni* is the most important of the pre-wedding rituals; it signifies the importance of the alliance of two families. It begins with *ardas* recited by the *granthi* who prays for God's blessing on the alliance of the two families. The ritual begins with the *milni* of the fathers of the bride and groom; now the bride's father makes a ritual gift of one turban and some cash to the groom's father. It is followed by the *milni* of maternal uncles. Similarly, the bride's uncle makes a ritual gift of one turban and some cash to his counterpart. Usually a list of important relatives is prepared by the groom's family who also receive a gift of a turban and some cash.

The ritual of *milni* is restricted to those kinsmen who are related to the family through blood or marriage, i.e. a grandfather, father's brother, father's sister's husband and a son-in-law. Friends of the groom's family do not receive any gifts; it signifies the nature of the ritual of *milni* as a boundary line between kin and other relationships.

A Sikh wedding in progress: (*top*) the bride and groom walk round the Adi Granth four times. (*above*) Bride and groom sit in front of the Adi Granth and are joined together with a pink scarf (*palla*) for the wedding ceremony.

ANAND KARAJ (WEDDING CEREMONY)

After the *milni* ceremony, the guests are entertained with a traditional Punjabi breakfast. Now the *barat* and other guests move to the gurdwara for the *anand karaj* ceremony at which the presence of the Adi Granth is mandatory. Bride and groom sit before the Adi Granth. *Anand karaj* begins with *ardas* followed by the ritual of *palla pharana* (joining the couple with the scarf worn by the groom); it is performed by the bride's father. This is a very emotional ritual in which the father gives away his daughter as a *kanayadan* (gift of a virgin). At this stage the *ragis* (religious musicians) sing the hymn of *palley taindey lagi* from the Adi Granth which stresses the permanence of the marital bond. The essence of this hymn is a pledge by the bride:

> Praise and blame I forsake both. I hold the edge of your garment/scarf. All else I let pass. All relationships I have found false. I cling to thee my lord. (AG 963)

LAVAN (WEDDING HYMN)

Now the reading and singing of the verses of the *lavan* from the Adi Granth begins. After the reading of each verse the couple walk round the Adi Granth in a clockwise direction, the bridegroom leading the bride. The circumambulation is repeated four times. The ceremony of *anand karaj* concludes with the recital of the hymn *anand sahib* and *ardas*.

A registry wedding is regarded only as a legal requirement. After the wedding ceremony, guests are entertained with a lavish meal. Usually, Sikh receptions are held at community centres or hotels.

DOLI (RITUAL DEPARTURE OF BRIDE WITH HER HUSBAND)

After lunch the ritual *doli torna* takes place. *Doli* is a kind of sedan in which the bride is carried to her husband's home by four *jheers* (water-carrier caste) men. The ritual of *doli torna* symbolizes permanent change in the bride's status from being a member of her father's household to being a member of her husband's clan; it is expressed in terms of being a *dhee* (daughter) to becoming a *noonh* (daughter-in-law). Nowadays, bride and groom leave in a car; the traditional role of the water-carriers has become redundant.

MUKLAWA

The consummation of marriage is called *muklawa*. In the Punjab a few years used to elapse between wedding and *muklawa*, depending on the age of the couple. In the UK and abroad, it usually takes place one day after the wedding. The daughter then departs permanently from her father's home. After the marriage a woman is expected to produce children, particularly sons in order to inherit their father's property and social status within the *biradari*. Nowadays, many couples go away for their honeymoon.

Dowry

Dowry is called *daaj* in Punjabi/Sikh society. Although the *Rahit Maryada* (Sikh code of discipline) declared the demanding and giving of dowries to be against Sikh teaching, the dowry system is still very popular among Sikhs. There is a fundamental difference between the traditional Hindu dowry system and Sikh practice; Sikhs do not ask or pay the bridegroom price.

A Sikh dowry refers to all gifts that are given to the bride at the wedding; it also includes gifts given to the groom and his relatives. Most Sikh parents provide a substantial amount of clothes, furniture, household goods and jewellery. In the Sikh diaspora, most Sikh brides are working women, and save a lot of money towards their own dowry. It used to be customary to show the dowry to the groom's father and his close relatives before it was packed. Nowadays, the practice of displaying a dowry has become very unpopular.

DIVORCE AND REMARRIAGE

Sikh marriage is regarded as a spiritual relationship; strictly speaking, therefore, there is no place for divorce or the breaking of the bond established in the presence of the Adi Granth. However, in 1955 the Indian parliament passed the Hindu Marriage Act which provides for divorce for Hindus, including Sikhs.

Despite this legislation, the rate of divorce among Sikhs is very low indeed, both in India and the diaspora. In the UK, Sikhs are governed by the marriage and divorce laws of the land. The incidence of divorce is on the increase among young Sikhs, though it is very low compared to the national statistics. Divorce continues to be regarded as a stigma, particularly on the honour of a woman and her family. A divorced woman is called *chhadi hoyi* (discarded woman).

Sikhs, however, practise the remarriage of both divorcees and widows. The remarriage of a widow is called *kareva/chadar-pauna*. In earlier times it was common practice to marry the widow of one's elder brother in order to protect the honour of the family. In this ceremony a groom marries a widow by placing a sheet of cloth (*chadar*) over her head in the presence of relatives and members of the *biradari*. A widow is not entitled to a religious wedding (*anand karaj*) because she cannot be given away as a *kanyadan* (gift of a virgin). Young widows move back to their parents who may arrange remarriage, while widows with children usually stay with their in-laws.

DEATH

Death is perceived as an ultimate reality in the Sikh tradition. A number of phrases are applied to describe the death of a person: *rab da bhana* (Divine Will), *pura ho giya* (completed his/her span of life), *surgwas ho giya* (has taken his/her abode in heaven) and *sansar yatra puri kar giya* (has completed the pilgrimage of this world). Sikhs believe in the doctrine of the transmigration of the soul, thus death is regarded as a gradual transition from the human state to another state, depending upon one's conduct in this world. Although the human body is cremated, the soul is believed to be immortal.

ANTAM-ISHNAN (LAST BATH)

In India, funerals usually take place soon after death or the next day depending on the timing of death. The ritual of *antam-ishnan* is performed before the body is carried to the cremation ground. The last bath is symbolic of the ritual purification of the body before cremation which is called *agni-bhaint* (offering to the god of fire)

AGNI-BHAINT

The bier is carried by the sons and brothers of the deceased, led by the chief mourner, the eldest son. The ritual of carrying the bier is called *modha-dena*. Women are forbidden to take part in this ritual. It is the ritual duty of a son to light the pyre. In the absence of a son one of his male relatives performs the ritual of lighting the pyre.

Before lighting the pyre, a *granthi* recites *ardas* for the departed soul. Women are prohibited from taking part in carrying the bier and lighting the pyre. In fact, they do not enter the cremation ground. At the death of a *sohagan* (married woman), her shroud is provided by her parental family, and she is dressed as a bride.

In the Punjab, the ashes are collected after three days and then deposited either in the river Ganges at Hardwar or at Kiratpur. Ritual gifts of clothes, utensils and some cash is offered to a family Brahmin for his services.

PAGRI (RITUAL TRANSFER OF PATERNAL AUTHORITY)

After the funeral, the deceased's family organize the reading of the Adi Granth either at their residence or local gurdwara. Usually, the reading of the Adi Granth marks the culmination of thirteen days of mourning, after which a big feast (akath) is held for the relatives and members of one's biradari.

The ritual of pagri (literally a turban) takes place at this time. The ceremony involves the chief mourner who sits in front of the scriptures and receives a turban and some cash from his maternal uncle. Then he wears the new turban in the presence of the relatives and members of the biradari, discarding the old one. Thereafter, he is reminded of his new status and responsibilities by a senior member of the biradari. He now joins the elders of the biradari for a communal meal, having been ritually accepted as the head of his household. The social function of the rite of pagri is to facilitate the gradual incorporation of a son into the role of his father.

WIDOWHOOD (RANDEYPA)

In Punjabi/Sikh society a widow is called vidhwa or randi. The term randi is very derogatory; it is used as a swear-word for wicked women and prostitutes; it also signifies the differential status of a widow in Punjabi/Indian society. At the death of her husband, she discards her colourful clothes and wears a white chuni (long scarf) that signifies the status of widowhood and a state of being in mourning.

On the thirteenth day following the death of a husband his widow is given a ritual bath by the ladies of the household. She discards her old clothes and wears a new set of clothes provided by her parental family. Now she discards her white scarf and she is ritually reincorporated into the family. Widows are not encouraged to take part in auspicious ceremonies such as wedding rituals.

ADOPTION

Traditionally, the adoption of children has been closely linked with the inheritance of property. A childless couple would adopt a male child of their close relations with a view to facilitating the transfer of their property. The fostering of children as understood in British and American society is virtually unknown in the Punjab. The nearest equivalent is the bringing up of orphan children belonging to one's extended family or close relatives.

ABORTION AND CONTRACEPTION

Life is regarded as a gift of God and is most sacred in Sikh teachings. In traditional Punjabi society abortion was never discussed publicly. In the event of an unmarried girl becoming pregnant, an abortion was procured to protect the honour of the family. When abortion is prescribed on medical grounds, Sikhs generally follow medical advice. Sikh children born and educated in Britain believe in family planning just like their British counterparts.

9 Sikh Sects

Namdhari Sikh musician and sons

After the death of Gobind Singh in 1708, the Sikh movement went through a period of unprecedented change. For example, in 1710 Sikhs established a sovereign state in the Punjab under the leadership of Banda Bahadur. Although Banda's rule lasted for only a short period of six years, it paved the way for the establishment of a Punjabi/Sikh state under the leadership of Maharaja Ranjit Singh in 1799. The Sikhs ruled Punjab for fifty years until it was annexed by the British in 1849.

The fifty-year period of independence brought peace and prosperity, and the Sikh hierarchy became enormously wealthy. One of the consequences was that some Sikhs not only lapsed into traditional ritualistic practices, but there were some others who converted to Christianity. Subsequently, the challenge of changed fortunes of the Sikhs in the post-annexation period gave birth to a number of reform movements

NAMDHARI SIKHS

Literally, Namdhari means one who upholds the name of God. The Namdhari movement was founded by Baba Balak Singh (1797-1862) from the town of Hazro, now in Pakistan. He appointed Ram Singh as his successor who transformed the movement into a dynamic socio-political force in the Punjab. The Namdhari movement played an important role in the struggle for Indian independence. In 1872, the British government deported Guru Ram Singh to Burma for causing unrest in the Punjab and sixty-six Namdhari Sikhs were executed by being tied to the mouths of cannons.

DISTINCTIVE FEATURES OF THE NAMDHARI SIKHS

1. According to Namdhari tradition, the tenth guru, Gobind Singh, did not die at Nander in 1708, but continued his mission under the name of Ajapal Singh and appointed Balak Singh as his successor.

2. Namdhari Sikhs believe in the continuity of the line of human gurus, although they have a very high regard for the Guru Granth Sahib. They also believe that Guru Ram Singh is still alive and will return from Burma to lead them.

3. All Namdharis are *amritdharis* (initiated Sikhs). They wear white clothes and are strict vegetarians. The style of their turban is called *sidhi-pagri* (laid flat across the forehead).

4. Namdhari Sikhs practise the system of arranged marriage but they prefer to choose spouses from Namdhari families.

5. At a Namdhari wedding, the bride and groom walk round the *havan* (holy fire) while the *lawan* (wedding hymns) are recited from the Adi Granth. Namdhari brides do not cover their faces.

6. The headquarters of the Namdhari movement is located at Bhaini Sahib, birthplace of Guru Ram Singh.

7. They use a woollen rosary (*mala*) during meditation.

8. Namdhari Sikhs do not fly the *nishan-sahib* (Sikh flag) over their gurdwaras.

Namdhari Sikhs have established their gurdwaras in many countries. At the present time, Satguru Jagjit Singh regularly visits his followers abroad.

NIRANKARI SIKHS

The Nirankari movement was founded by Baba Dyal Das during the period of Sikh rule in the Punjab. Nirankari literally means one who believes in the formless God. Baba Dyal Das was born in 1783 and died in 1854. He had witnessed the gradual process of ritualistic practices creeping in among the Sikhs, who, according to Baba Dyal Das, had forgotten the

teachings of Guru Nanak. He preached the purification of Sikh practice by insisting upon righteous
conduct rather than meaningless rituals.

Baba Dyal Das made a significant contribution
towards the simplification of Sikh rites of passage.
The Nirankaris consistently fought for the right to
solemnize the Sikh wedding in the presence of the Adi
Granth and the recital of *lawan* (wedding hymns from
the Adi Granth). Nirankaris also believe in the
necessity of a human guru.

RADHASOAMI MOVEMENT

The founder of the Radhasoami movement was Baba
Shiv Dyal. He was born in 1818 and died in 1878.
He was greatly influenced by the teachings of the Adi
Granth. The Radhasoami movement attracted a large
number of Sikhs when Jaimal Singh, a disciple of
Baba Shiv Dyal, established his headquarters at Beas
in the Punjab.

Radhasoamis believe in a living guru. They do not
install the Adi Granth or any other scriptures at their
place of worship. At their service, called *satsang*,
their guru sits on a raised platform and preaches from
a selection of hymns taken from the Adi Granth as
well as from compositions of other *Sants* (saints). Their
teachings are strictly anti-caste and they have
attracted a large number of untouchables to the
Radhasoami movement.

Radhasoamis are strict vegetarians. They do not
distribute *karah-parshad* at the end of their service.
Usually, they sit on chairs during their *satsang*

sessions, and do not insist on covering their heads or taking off their shoes. Since their guru lives at the *dera* (headquarters) in Beas, it has become an important place of pilgrimage for the Radhasoamis. They have built a modern hospital at Beas where a number of overseas Radhasoami doctors provide free service for a couple of weeks every year. The Radhasoami movement has attracted a significant number of educated people who are mainly responsible for the overall organization of the movement.

THE 3H ORGANIZATION

The 3H organization (healthy, happy, holy), also known as the Sikh Dharma Brotherhood, is the most interesting development within the Sikh movement in North America. It was founded in 1971 by Harbhajan Singh Puri, popularly known as Yogi Bhajan. He attracted a significant number of white Americans to Sikhism. They claim to have more than one hundred centres in North America and 250,000 people involved in their activities.

Members of the Sikh Dharma Brotherhood are *amritdharis* (initiated Sikhs). They follow the *Khalsa* code of discipline very strictly. Both men and women wear turbans; they usually wear white clothes. A number of white American Sikhs have learnt *shabad-kirtan* (religious singing) and accompany their leader, Yogi Bhajan, when he travels abroad. They perform *shabad-kirtan* at local gurdwaras. Although Punjabi Sikhs admire their dedication and commitment to Sikh teachings, they still call them 'gora' (white) Sikhs.

10 Sikh Diaspora

Sikh procession marking the Baisakhi festival

The presence of Sikh communities beyond the boundaries of the Punjab, particularly overseas, is one of the more remarkable episodes in human relations that has occurred over the last 150 years. The pattern of Sikh migration is inseparably linked with the British rule in India and freedom of movement within the British empire. After the Anglo-Sikh Wars, the annexation of the Punjab by the British in 1849 was one of the determining factors that prompted the wave of Sikh emigration. A large number of Sikh soldiers were recruited into the British Indian army, particularly after the mutiny of 1857. They were mainly drawn from the agricultural community popularly known as the *Jats*, and were entrusted to safeguard the interests of British empire both in India and abroad.

While serving in the armed forces, Sikh soldiers were able to obtain a personal knowledge of the potential economic opportunities in various parts of the British empire. Not surprisingly, therefore, after demobilization, many of them went back and settled in such places as Singapore, Hong Kong and Malaya, serving in the police force and as security guards etc. Some of them emigrated to Australia, Fiji, and Canada. These pioneer Sikh migrants were the main source of information for their relatives and friends in the Punjab that resulted in the chain migration of Sikhs. For example, nearly five thousand male Sikh migrants arrived in Canada between 1904 and 1907 before the Canadian Government imposed restrictions on the entry of immigrants from the sub-continent of India.

MIGRATION TO EAST AFRICA

The annexation of the Punjab in 1849 also opened up enormous opportunities for Sikh craftsmen popularly known as *Tarkhans* (carpenters, blacksmiths and bricklayers) both in India and abroad. The second most important wave of migration from the Punjab was that of the Sikh craftsmen who went to East Africa in the early twentieth century. Most significantly, they were recruited as indentured labour to build the Uganda-Kenya railway in the early twentieth century. According to Parminder Bhachu: 'Recruitment of labour from the Punjab in particular started in 1897. This carried on till 1901, during which period 32,000 Indian workers were recruited.'

The migration of Sikhs to East Africa continued until 1950, albeit with some immigration restrictions. But as there were no restrictions on bringing spouses from the Punjab, by the 1960s a vibrant Sikh community had developed in East Africa. By this time, many Sikhs were working in banks, post offices and the police force and their second generation had begun entering the professions, becoming teachers, doctors, lawyers and accountants. Some of them became highly successful building contractors and owners of garages all over East Africa.

MIGRATION TO BRITAIN

Although a small number of Sikh pioneer migrants had come to the UK before the Second World War, a mass migration of Sikhs began in the 1950s and early 1960s. There were no restrictions on the entry of British subjects and citizens of the New Commonwealth until the passing of the Commonwealth Immigration Act of 1962 which controlled the entry of male migrants. The main reasons for coming to Britain included pressure on the land and the shortage of industrial jobs in India, combined with a labour shortage in Britain coinciding with a boom in the British economy after the Second World War. Jobs, mostly unskilled, were not hard to find in the foundries and textile industry. In all, some 206,000 Sikhs emigrated to Britain during this period.

GURDWARAS IN THE DIASPORA

As we have seen, the gurdwara is one of the principal Sikh institutions which plays a central role in the everyday life of the Sikh community. As soon as there is a small number of Sikh residents in a town, they will take steps to establish a gurdwara which also becomes a central meeting place for them.

For example, East African Sikhs established their first gurdwara in Nairobi in 1900 and the first gurdwara in Canada in 1909 in Vancouver. In the Sikh diaspora, the gurdwara has emerged not only as a place of worship but also a centre for social activities, e.g. weddings and funeral services are conducted at the gurdwaras. Many gurdwaras also run Punjabi language and music classes for Sikh children.

Number of gurdwaras in the Sikh diaspora

UK (well over)	150	'Hong Kong	2
Canada	100	'Afganistan	10
USA	50	'Burma	4
Malaysia	57	'Iran	2
Thailand	9	'Iraq	1
Singapore	12	'France	1
Netherlands	1	'Denmark	1
Norway	1	'Sweden	1
Germany	6		

(N.S. Shergill 1985 quoted by Cole and Sambhi 1995: 189/192)

Sikh population

Punjab	12 million
Other parts of India	6 million
Outside India	2 million
Total population	20 million

(These figures are based on the national Census of India, 1991)

Estimated population of Sikhs in the diaspora

UK	600,000	(La Brack 1989:272)
Canada	250,000	(Dusenbery 1989:7)
USA	100,000	(. . . . .)
Australia	7,795	(National Census 1991)

INTEGRATION

The Sikh community in the diaspora has passed through many phases. By now, Sikhs have been living away from the Punjab for more than ten decades. From being single male migrants they have become settlers living in family households. They are no longer working purely as unskilled labourers but there has been a significant shift in their employment and occupational pattern.

Although youngsters' commitment to their parents' culture seems to be equally strong, their vision of Sikh traditional culture is quite different from that of the first-generation immigrants. Their attitude of questioning the traditional values is generally perceived as a threat to their authority by the parents, some of whom feel as if they have lost control over their children.

Interestingly, most Sikh parents regard the education of their children as a family investment and an instrument for enhancing their social status. A significant number of Sikh youngsters have gained professional qualifications, i.e. as doctors, dentists, lawyers, accountants, teachers, social workers and nurses. The number of Sikh children attending institutions of higher education is growing rapidly.

The Sikh community in the diaspora has displayed a remarkable capacity for adaptation and compromise. For example, the traditional mode of arranged marriage has given way to an 'assisted marriage'; now the spouses are introduced to each other and their consent is obtained before final approval of the relationship.

The degree of integration can be measured by looking at the way the Sikh community is integrating into the host society's culture while retaining its distinctive identity. Although participation in gurdwara activities is a major attraction, a number of Sikhs are actively involved in main-stream politics. For example, a number of Sikhs have been elected as local authority councillors and a few have been elected as lord mayors. At present, there are two Sikh Members of Parliament at Westminster. Likewise, one Sikh, Ujjal Singh Dosanjh, has become the first Attorney-General and Minister for Multiculturalism in British Columbia, Canada.

The Sikh flag – *Nishan Sahib*

APPENDIX 1

Hymns from the Adi Granth

He, who calls himself a disciple of the True Guru
Let him rise early in the morning and contemplate the Lord's Name.
Let him attune himself to the Lord and bathe in the pool of nectar at the early hour.
Let him dwell upon the Lord through the Guru's Word that all his sins are washed off.
And when the sun rises, let him sing the Guru's Word, and reflect on the Lord's Name, upstanding and downsitting.
He who contemplates my Lord with every breath, he, the devotee, becomes the beloved of the Guru.
He on whom the Lord's mercy, him alone He instructs the Guru's wisdom.
Nanak craves the dust of the devotee's feet who contemplates himself and makes others contemplate the Name of the Lord.

(Adi Granth 305-6)

Thy Name, O Lord, is the dispeller of sorrow,
So I dwell on the Wisdom of the Perfect Guru, night and day.
The heart in which abides the Supreme Lord, is a beauteous place.
He, whose tongue utters the Lord's praise, the *yama* couriers touch him not.
I was awake not to the service of the Lord, nor did I dwell upon Him.
But Thou art (in the end) my only refuge. O Life of all life, O Infinite, Unknowable Thou!
When Thou, the Lord of the earth, art in mercy, hasten away all my sorrows;
And even the hot winds touch me not and Thou keepest me whole.

The Guru is the Lord, the God, The true Creator.
When He, the Guru, is beneficent, I receive all His bounties.
Says Nanak, 'I am a sacrifice unto my Lord, the God'.

(Adi Granth 218)

I would love to be a deer, abiding in the woods, and living on the roots,
If by the Guru's grace, thus do I meet my Lord unto whom I am a sacrifice.
I am the pedlar of my Lord, and deal only in the merchandise of His Name.
I would be a *Koel*, sheltered in a mango grove, and dwell in peace, on the Word.
If thus do I meet my Lord of indescribable beauty, the natural way.
I would be a fish, abiding in water, if thus do I remember the Lord who supports all;
And hug Him, in a close embrace, and see him here, there and everywhere.
I would be a serpent living under the ground,
If thus would the (music of the) Word charm me to make me fear-free.
Nanak: he alone for ever is blest whose soul merges in the All-Soul.

(Adi Granth 157)

He who is pained not by pain,
Nor affected by pleasure, nor affection, nor fear; and gold to him is as dust;
And who is swayed neither by praise nor dispraise, nor by greed, attachment, or ego,
And who rises above both joy and sorrow and honour, dishonour;
And forsakes hope and desire and remains detached from the world:
And whom lust and wrath visit not: within him abides God.
He on whom is the Guru's Grace, he alone knows the way.
Says Nanak, 'He merges in God, as water mingles with water'.

(Adi Granth 633-34)

(From the *Sri Guru Granth Sahib (English Version)*, translated and annotated by Dr Gopal Singh, 1987. New Delhi: World Sikh Centre Inc.)

Glossary

Adi Granth: Sacred scripture of the Sikhs, also called *Guru Granth Sahib*.

akal: Timeless, a term used to describe God.

akal takhat: Literally the throne of the Timeless God. It was built by the sixth Guru, Hargobind, facing the Golden Temple, Amritsar.

akhand path: Unbroken reading of the *Adi Granth* taking forty-eight hours.

amrit: Nectar of immortality; solution of water and sugar used at the Sikh initiation ceremony.

amritdhari: An initiated Sikh.

anand Karaj: The Sikh wedding ceremony.

ardas: Sikh prayer recited at the conclusion of a service.

baba: Literally a grandfather, a term of respect applied to holy men.

Baisakhi: New Year's Day in the Punjab, the first day of the month of Baisakh, one of the principal festivals of the Sikhs, anniversary of the founding of the *Khalsa*.

bani: Compositions of the Gurus and other saints included in the Sikh scriptures.

bhai: Literally a brother, title of respect accorded to men of piety and learning; also used for the custodian of a *gurdwara*.

bhakti: Religious devotion or worship.

bichola: A match-maker.

biradari: A punjabi term which refers to both the brotherhood and members of a caste group.

bura pauna: A post-funeral rite performed at the death of a husband; a widow receives ritual gifts from her parental family.

chamar: A leather worker; a term also used for members of the *Chamar* caste group.

chamardli: Residential area reserved for the *Chamars*.

chanini: a fringed awning fixed over the *Adi Granth*.

charan pahul: Literally foot initiation; water touched by the toe of the *guru* and used for the initiation ceremony. The Sikh method of initiation until it was replaced by the tenth Guru, Gobind Singh, in 1699.

chauri: A ritual fan made of Yak hair or peacock feathers; it is waved over the *Adi Granth*; symbol of authority.

daaj: Dowry.

daan: Charitable gifts for which no return is expected.

Dasam Granth: A collection of writings attributed to the tenth Guru, Gobind Singh.

Dharmsala: Commonly a term applied to a building used for devotional singing and worship; in the early Sikh period it was used to describe the Sikh place of worship.

Diwali: Festival of lights celebrated by Hindus and Sikhs in the month of October-November.

giani/gyani: A person well-read in Sikh scriptures.

granth: Book, a volume.

Granthi: A Sikh who looks after the *Adi Granth*; a reader of the *Adi Granth*, may also be a custodian of a *gurdwara*.

grihasthi: A householder; a term used for the second stage of life in Hinduism.

gurmata: Literally a *guru's* intention; a resolution approved by the Sikh congregation in the presence of the *Adi Granth*.

gurmukh: *Guru*-oriented person.

gurmukhi: Literally from *guru's* mouth; script used for writing Punjabi; the *Adi Granth* is written in *Gurmukhi* script.

guru: Religious teacher or a perceptor; one who delivers a disciple from ignorance.

Guru Granth Sahib: a term used for the *Adi Granth* since the death of the tenth Guru, Gobind Singh, symbolizing the end of human guruship.

hayan: Fire worship; popular among the *Namdhari* Sikhs.

Hola: Sikh festival held at Anandpur.

hukamnama: A hymn read out from the *Adi Granth* at the culmination of a service.

kachha/kachhaira: A pair of breeches worn by the *amritdhari* Sikhs; one of the Five Ks.

kangha: A small wooden comb, one of the Five Ks.

kara: Steel bracelet worn on the right wrist, one of the Five Ks.

kaur: Literally a princess; name assumed by female Sikhs after initiation.

karah-parshad: Blessed food which is distributed at the culmination of a Sikh service.

kes/kesh: Uncut hair, one of the Five Ks.

Khalsa: The Sikh Order instituted by the tenth Guru, Gobind Singh, in 1699.

khanda: A double-edged sword, one of the Sikh emblems.

kirpan: A sword, one of the Five Ks.

kirtan/shabad kirtan: Singing of hymns from the *Adi Granth*.

langar: Communal meal served at the culmination of a Sikh service; also used for a kitchen attached to every *gurdwara*.

manmukh: A self-oriented person.

masand: Authorized leaders of local Sikh communities appointed by the Sikh *Gurus* before the founding of the *Khalsa*.

milni: Customary meeting of the heads of families before the wedding ceremony.

mona: Clean-shaven.

namdhari: Literally upholder of the *Nam*. A Sikh movement initiated by Guru Ram Singh; *Namdhari* Sikhs believe in a living *guru*.

nishan sahib: A Sikh flag.

pag/pagri: A turban.

panj kakke: Five Ks.

panj pyarey: The original members of the *Khalsa*; literally beloved five.

panth: A term applied to the Sikh society.

ragi: Literally a musician; a term used for the Sikh musicians.

Ramgarhia: A Sikh artisan caste comprising of carpenters, blacksmiths and brick-layers.

Sahajdhari: A Sikh who may or may not wear outward symbols.

salwar-kameez: Literally baggy trousers and tunic; traditional Punjabi wear for women.

sangat: Sikh congregation.

sat sri akal: Sikh greeting.

sewa: Voluntary service.

Shiromani Gurdwara Parbandhak Committee: The committee which controls historic *gurdwaras* in the Punjab.

Sikh: Literally a learner, a student or a disciple; a term used for members of the Sikh community.

takhat: Literally a throne; a term used for five historic *gurdwaras* in India.

Waheguru: Wonderful Lord; a Sikh term for God.

Further Reading

Barrier, N.G. and Dusenbery, V.A. (eds.) (1989) *The Sikh Diaspora: Migration and the Experience Beyond Punjab*. Delhi: Chanakya Publications.

Barrow, Joy (ed.) (1998) *Meeting Sikhs*. Leicester: Christian Aware.

Cole, W.O. and Sambhi, P.S. (1995) *The Sikhs: Their Religious Beliefs and Practices*. Brighton: Sussex Academic Press.

Kalsi, S.S. (1992) *The Evolution of a Sikh Community in Britain*. Department of Theology and Religious Studies, University of Leeds.

McLeod, W.H. (1997) *Sikhism*. London: Penguin Books.

O'Connell, J.T., Israel, M. and Oxtoby, W.G. (eds.) (1988) *Sikh History And Religion in the Twentieth Century*. Toronto: University of Toronto.

Singh, Harbans (1985) *Heritage of the Sikhs*. Delhi: Manohar Publications.

Singh, Khushwant (1963) *A History of the Sikhs*, Vol.1, 1469-1839. Princeton: Princeton University Press.

—, (1991) *A History of the Sikhs*, Vol.2, 1839-1988. Delhi: Oxford University Press.

Index

Note: See Glossary for Punjabi terms